# FENG CROCHET

# FENG CROCHET

## CALMING PROJECTS FOR A HARMONIOUS HOME

*Nikki Van De Car*

RUNNING PRESS
PHILADELPHIA

Published by Running Press,
An Imprint of Perseus Books, LLC,
A Subsidiary of Hachette Book Group, Inc.

Printed in China

Books published by Running Press are available at special discounts for
bulk purchases in the United States by corporations, institutions, and
other organizations. For more information, please contact the Special
Markets Department at Perseus Books, 2300 Chestnut Street, Suite
200, Philadelphia, PA 19103, or call (800) 810-4145, ext. 5000, or
e-mail special.markets@perseusbooks.com.

ISBN 978-0-7624-6262-9
Library of Congress Control Number: 2017941322

E-book ISBN 978-0-7624-6263-6

9  8  7  6  5  4  3  2  1
Digit on the right indicates the number of this printing

Edited by Shannon Lee Connors
Tech edited by Therese Chynoweth
Designed by Susan Van Horn
Prop styling by Kristi Hunter
Typography: Brandon Text, Artisania, and Naive
Running Press thanks Lisa Stockbrand, at whose home many of these
photos were taken.

Running Press Book Publishers
2300 Chestnut Street
Philadelphia, PA 19103-4371

Visit us on the web!
www.runningpress.com

# CONTENTS

# INTRODUCTION

Our homes are meant to be a refuge. We go out to work, to shop, to exercise—all important and (hopefully) pleasurable things. But sometimes, for one reason or another, it feels more like we go out to do battle. We get stuck in traffic, we wait in lines, we argue with colleagues, we struggle to meet deadlines . . . and when we come home at the end of the day, we are exhausted and depleted.

At times like that, it is essential that the place we come home to can provide us with peace, with calm, with nurturing and healing support. Feng Shui—which is simply the interaction between you and your environment—is meant to help you achieve success in your life, however you define it. Depending on how you create that environment, by how decorate your home, you can bring yourself into harmony with the natural flow of energy around you, bringing you more energy in turn.

The stress and anxiety of our daily lives are prompting many of us to seek the elements of the natural world, to find peace. We can bring nature indoors, make it a part of our home, turning our surroundings into something beautiful and nurturing. This beomes doubly powerful when you create that haven yourself. Just the act of making provides a reflective release, as you tap into your creativity and your ability to bring something into the world, where before there was nothing.

The patterns in this book are all inspired by the philosophies and practices of Feng Shui, and thus they are all simple, meditative, and beautiful. As you bring table runners, mandala coasters, and cotton plant hangers into your home, you will create that refuge you crave, so that you can find the peace and restorative happiness you need.

# ABOUT FENG SHUI

At its heart, Feng Shui is a very simple practice. It is the act of bringing your surroundings into harmony with nature—both our own, internal nature and the natural world. "Feng Shui" translates to "wind-water," highlighting two of the five elements (Wood, Fire, Earth, Metal, and Water) that the art of Feng Shui holds in balance.

There are three core principles at work within Feng Shui: the elements, qi (which translates to "energy," or "life-force"), and the bagua, which is a map of your home, featuring principles like abundance, career, family, and so forth—all the things we negotiate in our homes, throughout our lives. When you dive into Feng Shui, it becomes quite complex—there's a reason there are certified practitioners offering guidance for those of us who aren't quite sure we understand all the principles. I make no pretenses about being one of those certified practitioners! This book offers only a small glimpse into the workings of Feng Shui, just to give you an idea of how to get started.

For all practical purposes, *Feng Crochet* focuses on just the five elements, giving you ideas, thoughts, and patterns for ways to incorporate those five elements into your home.  But *how* you incorporate those elements depends on qi, and on the bagua, and each of those elements affects the others.

Everything has energy. That chair you love, even though it might be a little faded and ratty, because it's just so comfortable and comforting? That's positive energy, free-flowing qi. But that end table you inherited from your grandmother, that you *ought* to love but just makes you sad—its energy just isn't working for you. It's blocked, and the qi within your home is blocked by it. You want to balance these kinds of energies, as well as the energies of the elements and the bagua, so that the qi within your home flows gently, ebbing and flowing in a peaceful, natural rhythm.

Each of these sections represents an area in your home, and an area of your life to focus on in that space. Each section resonates with a particular element. The center of the bagua—and the center of your home—represents a healthy state, where all of your elements, and all of the different demands you place on yourself, are in balance.

Now, most of our houses are not octagonal, so this is a very rough guide. You can use the bagua in whatever way feels the most natural to you; if there is a room in a southeasterly part of your house that would make a good home office, terrific! If you can put your bedroom in the southwest corner, that's great, too. And if some of these parts of life feel less important to you than others—if fame is less important than health and creativity, for example then feel free to minimize those parts. This is about *your* qi, about *your* home, and it should reflect you.

# bagua diagram

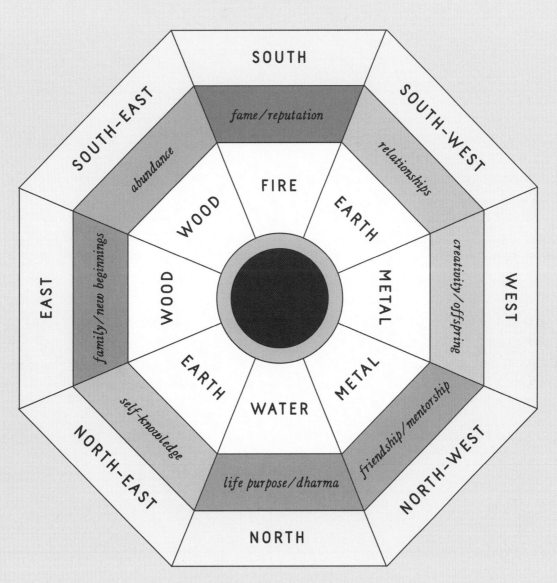

SOUTH

SOUTH-EAST

SOUTH-WEST

fame/reputation

abundance

relationships

FIRE

WOOD

EARTH

WOOD

METAL

EAST

family/new beginnings

WEST

creativity/offspring

EARTH

METAL

WATER

self-knowledge

friendship/mentorship

NORTH-EAST

life purpose/dharma

NORTH-WEST

NORTH

# WOOD

THE WOOD ELEMENT HELPS TO PROMOTE GROWTH AND CREATIVITY. If you're looking to expand your intuition, to be more imaginative, or to grow as a person, incorporating some Wood into your home will help move that process along.

That can be as simple as buying a houseplant. But for a more creative take on Feng Shui, the color green enhances the Wood element, as does anything tall and vertical. Thin, rectangular shapes like the bookmark and table runner work well with the Wood element, and created leaves like the dishcloths remind us of growth and imagination, even while doing something as mundane as washing up after dinner.

On the bagua map, Wood can be found in Family and New Beginnings and in Abundance, both parts of our lives that we need to nurture and grow. The Wood element is nourished by Water, and it is controlled by Metal. If you're looking to bring more Wood into your home, be sure to complement it with Water, and perhaps tone down the Metal.

# stool cover

*This homey cover highlights the plainest piece of furniture of all—the humble stool. Stools are practical and rustic, and sometimes it's good to put our attention on the simple things in life.*

*This pattern is written for a stool with an 11-inch/28-cm diameter seat, but it is easily adjustable.*

. . . . . . . . . . . . . . . . . . . . . . . . . . . . . . . . . . . . . . . . . . . . . . . . . . . . . .

## FINISHED MEASUREMENTS

13¼ inches (33.5 cm) diameter.

## MATERIALS

130 yards (119 meters) worsted weight cotton yarn (shown in Noro Tokonatsu, in color #22 Pistachio, 1 skein)

Size H-8 (5 mm) crochet hook, or size needed to obtain gauge

Safety pin or locking stitch marker

Tapestry needle

## GAUGE

12 sts and 6 rnds = 4 inches (10 cm) in pattern rnds 4–6.

## PATTERN

Foundation ring: Ch 4, join in the rnd with a sl st in first ch to form a ring.

**Rnd 1**: Ch 1, work 8 sc around ring, join with a sl st in top of first sc. Place a safety pin to mark the beginning of the rnd—8 sts.

**Rnd 2**: Ch 2, 2 dc in base of beginning ch, 3 dc in each st around, join with a sl st in top of beginning ch—24 sts.

**Rnd 3**: Ch 1, hdc in base of beginning ch, *ch 1, skip 1, 2 hdc in next st; repeat from * around, join with a sl st in top of beginning ch—24 sts and 12 ch-sp.

**Rnd 4**: Ch 2, 5 dc in ch-sp, 6 dc in each remaining ch-sp around, join with a sl st in top of beginning ch—72 sts.

**Rnd 5**: Ch 2, dc in each st around.

**Rnd 6**: Ch 1, hdc in next st, *ch 1, skip 1, dc in each of next 2 sts; repeat from * around, join with a sl st in top of beginning ch—48 sts and 24 ch-sp.

Repeat rnds 4–6 until your piece is the diameter of your stool when slightly stretched. It doesn't matter which rnd you end on.

Repeat rnd 5 for 2 inches (5 cm). Fasten off.

## *finishing:*

Weave in all ends using a tapestry needle. Finish according to the instructions on page 101.

# plant hanger

This is the only pattern that literally brings wood into your home. Using a lot of the color green and making leaf-shaped or leaf-inspired items is all very well, but there isn't really a substitute for the living plant itself.

This plant hanger is strong, and the pattern is versatile enough so that you can make it to fit whatever pot, glass bowl or ball or vase you want—whatever sparks your sense of creativity!

## FINISHED MEASUREMENTS

12 inches (30.5 cm) circumference and 13½ inches (34.5 cm) long.

## MATERIALS

52 yards (47 meters) DK weight yarn (shown in Debbie Bliss Cotton DK, in color #13077 Mint, 1 ball)

Size H-8 (5 mm) crochet hook, or size needed to obtain gauge

Stitch marker

Tapestry needle

## GAUGE

13 sts and 13 rnds = 4 inches (10 cm) in single crochet.

## NOTES

This plant hanger is worked spirally in the round without joining at the end of each round. Use a locking stitch marker to mark the beginning of each round, and move the marker up as you work.

## PATTERN

**Foundation ring**: Ch 3, join in the rnd with a sl st in first ch to form a ring.

**Rnd 1**: Work 8 sc around ring—8 sts.

**Rnd 2**: Work 2 sc in each st around—number of sts is doubled.

**Rnd 3**: Work sc in each st around.

Repeat rnds 2 and 3 until your work is the size of the bottom of your planter, making sure you have a multiple of 4 sts.

### *sides:*

**Next rnd**: Ch 1, hdc in each st around.

Continue working hdc around until you can slip your entire planter inside. Check the length by flipping the planter upside down and sliding the hanger over the planter, pressing down around the sides to stretch it. Your sides are long enough when the sides are ½ inch (1.3 cm) from the top edge of the planter when stretched.

**Decrease rnd**: *Sc2tog, sc in next 2 sts; repeat from * around.

Count your sts. Are they divisible by 4? If so, work 1 round of sc. If not, sc around, decreasing as necessary to bring your stitch count to a number divisible by 4.

Sc one-quarter of the way around, make a ch 24 inches (61 cm) long, *sc in next st, then in each st one-quarter of the way around, make a ch 24 inches (61 cm) long; repeat from * 2 times more, join with a sl st in top of first sc. Fasten off.

### *finishing:*

Weave in all ends using a tapestry needle.

# table runner

*The interlocking gingko leaves of this runner bring a bright spark of green to your table. The Wood element represents life, energy, and growth, and gingko leaves in particular symbolize longevity. When your family gathers around the table for a special meal, like Thanksgiving or another celebration, this table runner can serve to remind everyone how the life of a family lasts through each generation.*

## FINISHED MEASUREMENTS

Approximately 52 inches (132 cm) long by 11½ inches (29 cm) wide.

This table runner can be made larger or smaller by working more or fewer leaves than the pattern calls for. Please note that, like a family, this runner is built from its individual parts. It can require a little attention to bring those parts together—again, like any family—but it's worth it.

## MATERIALS

350 yards (320 meters) sport weight yarn (shown in Madelinetosh Tosh Sport, in color Forestry, 2 hanks)

Size E-4 (3.5 mm) crochet hook

Size M-13 (9 mm) crochet hook

Tapestry needle

## GAUGE

Gauge is not critical to this pattern.

## PATTERN

Make 84 gingko leaves.

### gingko leaf:

**Foundation ring**: Using smaller crochet hook, ch 12, join in the rnd with a sl st in 6th ch from hook.

**Row 1**: Change to larger crochet hook. Ch 3, work 5 tr, dc, 6 tr around ring. Do not join. Fasten off.

### joining leaves:

Divide leaves into 2 piles of 42 leaves each.

*Using smaller crochet hook, join 2 leaves with a sl st at bottom of both stems, ch 9, join both leaves with a sl st in last dc of both leaves. Do not cut yarn.

Working with next 2 leaves, repeat from * until you have 21 pairs of 42 leaves attached along the chain. Fasten off.

Repeat with the remaining 42 leaves.

### joining chains:

Lay strips next to each other on a flat surface, with beginning of each strip nearest you. Using smaller crochet hook, join yarn to 4th tr of bottom 2 leaves of each strip, sl st in same st of both leaves, *ch 10, sl st in 4th tr of next 2 leaves; repeat from * until you've reached the top. Fasten off.

### finishing:

Join yarn to 4th tr of bottom outside leaf on right edge of runner, *ch 10, sl st in 4th tr of next leaf along edge; repeat from * to top leaf. Fasten off.

Repeat along left edge of runner.

Weave in all ends using a tapestry needle (you can weave them in two at a time to save yourself some trouble). Finish as directed on page 101, making sure your leaves are untwisted.

# throw pillow

*The little knobs of texture on this throw pillow call to mind knots in tree branches, or those little bumps that grow on leaves from time to time. It is soft and squishy and very simple, showing how a very small change in the pattern can make an enormous difference.*

## FINISHED MEASUREMENTS

18 inches (45.5 cm) square.

## MATERIALS

380 yards/347 meters Aran weight yarn (shown in Malabrigo Worsted, in color #MM056 Olive, 2 hanks)

Size F-5 (3.75 mm) crochet hook, or size needed to obtain gauge

Size K-10½ (6.5 mm) crochet hook

Tapestry needle

18 by 18 inch (45.75 by 45.75 cm) pillow form

## GAUGE

14½ sts and 18 rows = 4 inches (10 cm) in single crochet, using smaller crochet hook.

## NOTES

Puffs are worked using the larger crochet hook, and the remainder of the pillow is worked using the smaller crochet hook.

## *puff*

Using larger hook, [yarn over, insert hook in st, yarn over and draw through a loop] 3 times in same st (7 loops on hook), yarn over, draw through all loops on hook (1 loop on hook).

## PATTERN

### *front:*

**Foundation ch**: Using smaller hook, ch 65.

**Row 1**: Ch 1, sc in each ch across, turn.

**Rows 2–5**: Ch 1, sc in each st across, turn.

**Row 6**: Ch 1, sc in first 4 sts, *puff in next st, sc in next 7 sts; repeat from * to last 5 sts, puff in next st, sc in last 4 sts, turn.

**Row 7**: Ch 1, sc in each st and puff across, turn.

**Rows 8–9**: Repeat row 2, turn.

**Row 10**: Ch 1, sc in first 8 sts, puff, *sc in next 7 sts, puff; repeat from * to last 8 sts, sc to end of row, turn.

**Row 11–13**: Repeat row 7, turn.

Repeat rows 6–13 until piece measures 17 inches (43 cm), ending with row 6 or row 10.

Work 5 rows of sc. Fasten off.

### back:

**Foundation ch**: Using smaller crochet hook, ch 65.

**Row 1**: Ch 1, sc in each ch across, turn.

**Row 2**: Ch 1, sc in each st across, turn.

Repeat row 2 until piece measures 18 inches (45.5 cm). Fasten off.

### finishing:

Weave in all ends using a tapestry needle.

Holding both pieces together with WS together (RS facing out), and using smaller hook, work sc through both layers along 3 sides to join. Insert pillow and sc across remaining edge, then join with a sl st in top of first sc. Fasten off.

Weave in remaining ends using a tapestry needle.

# leaf dishcloths

*Thich Nhat Hanh tells us to "wash the dishes to wash the dishes." He asks us to view this "chore" as an act of mind-fulness, to be present. This is by no means an easy task. I know that when I'm washing the dishes, I'm eager to be done so I can go watch a movie, read a book, join in the conversation—or just be doing anything that isn't washing the dishes. But Thich Nhat Hanh reminds us that when we are in that state, the state of rushing to get to the next, "better" moment, we aren't living in this moment at all.*

*Use these dishcloths as a little reminder of the importance of all life, even the moments or chores that can seem tedious. If you can wash the dishes as if you are "bathing a baby Buddha," all of life can be miraculous.*

## FINISHED MEASUREMENTS

Approximately 4 inches (10 cm) wide and 6½ inches (16.5 cm) long, excluding hanger loop.

## MATERIALS

25 yards/23 meters DK weight yarn (shown in Debbie Bliss Cotton DK, in colors #13078 Jade [MC], #13077 Mint [CC1], and #13079 Citrus [CC2], 1 ball each)

Size G-6 (4 mm) crochet hook, or size needed to obtain gauge

Tapestry needle

## GAUGE

12 sts and 8 rows = 4 inches (10 cm) in double crochet.

## PATTERN

**Foundation ring**: Using MC, ch 3, join in the rnd with a sl st in first ch to form a ring.

**Row 1**: Ch 3 (counts as dc), work 4 dc around ring, ch 2 and turn (do not join)—5 sts.

**Increase row**: Dc in each st across to last st, 2 dc in top of beginning ch, ch 2 and turn—1 st increased.

Repeat increase row 5 times more—11 sts.

**Decrease row**: Skip first st, dc in each st across, ch 2 and turn—1 st decreased.

Repeat decrease row 3 times more—7 sts remain.

**Next row**: Dc2tog, dc in next 3 sts, dc2tog, ch 2 and turn—5 sts remain.

**Next row**: Dc2tog, dc, dc2tog, ch 2 and turn—3 sts remain.

**Next row**: Dc3tog—1 st remains. Fasten off.

## finishing:

Join CC of your choice to bottom of foundation ring, sl st around entire outer edge of leaf, ch 6, sl st to first sl st, creating a hanging loop. Sl st along center of leaf to top edge (it doesn't have to be perfectly straight). Cut yarn and pull tail through last st.

Weave in all ends using a tapestry needle.

# bookmark

*As books are made of paper, in a sense they are set apart from the Wood element—the wood in them is no longer alive; it is inert. A little green bookmark, with a leaf on either end, can counteract that sense. For no one could ever say that books aren't nourishing, or that a home filled with books could be anything less than peaceful and strong.*

## FINISHED MEASUREMENTS

Approximately 13 inches (33 cm) long.

## MATERIALS

20 yards (18 meters) fingering weight yarn (shown in Dream in Color Smooshy, in color Happy Forest, 1 hank)

Size F-5 (3.75 mm) crochet hook, or size needed to obtain gauge (see Gauge note)

Tapestry needle

## GAUGE

28 sts and 28 rows = 4 inches (10 cm) in single crochet.

Gauge is not critical for this pattern, though if your gauge is different, your finished measurements will not be the same.

## PATTERN

**Foundation ch**: Ch 3.

**Row 1**: Begin in 2nd ch from hook, sc in each ch across, ch 1 and turn—2 sts.

**Row 2**: Work 2 sc in each of next 2 sts, ch 1 and turn—4 sts.

**Row 3**: Sc in each st across, ch 1, and turn.

**Row 4**: 2 sc in first st, sc in next 2 sts, 2 sc in last st, ch 1 and turn—6 sts.

**Row 5**: Sc in each st across, ch 1 and turn.

**Row 6**: Sc2tog, sc in next 2 sts, sc2tog, ch 1 and turn—4 sts remain.

**Row 7**: [Sc2tog] twice, ch 1 and turn—2 sts remain.

**Row 8**: Sc2tog—1 st remains.

*Insert hook into next visible hole along center of leaf, yarn over and pull through loop on hook, creating a sl st; repeat from * down center to end of leaf.

Flip leaf over and repeat from * to create a "rib" along center of other side of leaf.

Tightly ch for 10¾ inches (27.5 cm).

**Foundation ch**: Turn, skip first ch, work 2 sc in each of next 2 ch, ch 1 and turn—4 sts.

**Row 1**: Work 2 sc in first st, sc in next 2 sts, 2 sc in last st, ch 1 and turn—6 sts.

**Row 2**: Sc in each st across, ch 1 and turn.

**Row 3**: Sc2tog, sc in next 2 sts, sc2tog, ch 1 and turn—4 sts remain.

**Row 4**: Sc in each st across, ch 1 and turn.

**Row 5**: [Sc2tog] twice, ch 1 and turn— 2 sts remain.

**Row 6**: Sc in each st across, ch 1 and turn.

**Row 7**: Sc2tog—1 st remains.

Work sl st along center of both sides of leaf same as for first leaf. Fasten off.

## *finishing:*

Weave in all ends using a tapestry needle.

Soak bookmark in lukewarm water for a few minutes. Squeeze to remove excess water, then lay flat to dry.

# FIRE

FIRE IS JOYFUL, ENERGETIC, AND TRANSFORMATIVE. IT CAN BE destructive, but a little brightness and heat is always a good thing. If you want to be more dynamic, have more energy, and perhaps live with a little more joy, try incorporating some of the Fire element into your home.

Fire's color is red, and its shape is a triangle, though anything pointed—like the star afghan—will bring Fire's energy into your space. But a candle or lampshade cover can draw attention to the literal fire and energy in your home, and curtain ties can let in the light. Anything red or orange will invoke Fire's energy, so simple stacking baskets will draw the eye, and the orange cast-iron handle cover will remind you of iron's heat and soften its hardness.

Unsurprisingly, Fire is what sets alight your Reputation and Fame bagua sector. Again, it's important to keep Fire under control, and perhaps balance it with some Water, but if you're really looking to bring more Fire into your life, complement it with some Wood, which will feed the Fire and make it burn more brightly.

# cast-iron handle cover

*Whenever I invite someone into my home, I cook for them. Brunches, dinner parties—these are wonderful ways to show friends and family how much we care. But sometimes the pressure to perform and impress (very Fire-like desires) causes me to lose track of what really matters, and I often burn myself—usually figuratively, but sometimes literally!*

*This cast-iron handle cover is a gentle reminder that the Fire element is meant to evoke warmth and liveliness, as we connect with the people who matter to us the most.*

## FINISHED MEASUREMENTS

Approximately 5¼ inches (13.5 cm) circumference and 4½ inches (11.5 cm) long.

## MATERIALS

50 yards (46 meters) worsted weight yarn (shown in Misti Alpaca Qolla Worsted, in color Maria, 1 hank)

Size H-8 (5 mm) crochet hook, or size needed to obtain gauge

Tapestry needle

## GAUGE

12 sts and 17 rnds = 4 inches (10 cm) in single crochet.

## PATTERN

**Foundation ch**: Ch 15, join in the rnd with a sl st in first ch to form a ring.

**Rnd 1**: Sc in each ch around—15 sts.

**Rnd 2**: Sc in each st around.

Repeat last rnd until piece measures 10 inches (25.5 cm) from beginning.

Fold cover in half, inserting one end into the tube, so that piece is twice as thick.

**Next rnd**: Work 1 rnd of sc through both layers to join edges, join with a sl st in first sc. Fasten off.

## *finishing:*

Weave in all ends using a tapestry needle.

# lampshade cover

*LED lightbulbs give me a headache. Their light is too harsh, too bright, and too cold—but I buy them because they are better for the environment, and they last forever. This lampshade cover brings some Fire back to the light in your home, adding light that warms as well as illuminates.*

*Adapt this pattern to suit the lampshade you have! It'll work for any type of round shade.*

. . . . . . . . . . . . . . . . . . . . . . . . . . . . . . .

## FINISHED MEASUREMENTS

For shade shown, 43 inches (109 cm) top circumference, 45 inches (114.5 cm) bottom circumference, and 11 inches (28 cm) tall.

## MATERIALS

255 yards (233 meters) worsted weight yarn (shown in Classic Elite Yarns Classic Silk, in color #6927 Cool Cranberry, 2 balls)

Size K-10½ (6.5 mm) crochet hook, or size needed to obtain gauge

Tapestry needle

## GAUGE

8 sts and 6¼ rnds = 4 inches (10 cm) in double crochet.

## NOTES

The amount of yarn you will need will vary with the size of the shade you're covering.

After the first round, the shade is worked in the round spirally, without joining at the end of each round.

## PATTERN

**Foundation ch**: Make a ch 2 inches (5 cm) smaller than top circumference (narrowest part) of your shade. For the cover shown, the circumference of the shade is 45 inches (114.3 cm), and the foundation ch is 88 sts.

**Row 1**: Begin in 2nd ch from hook and sc in each ch across. Join with a sl st in top of first sc, being careful not to twist.

**Rnd 1**: Ch 1, sc in each st around.

**Rnd 2**: Ch 2, dc tbl in each st around.

### *for a shade with a gentle slope:*

*Work 6 rnds even in dc.

**Inc rnd**: Work 2 dc in first sc, [dc one-quarter of the way around, 2 dc in next st] 3 times, dc in each st to end—4 sts increased.

Repeat from * until cover is desired length when stretched.

### *for a shade with a sharper slope:*

*Work 3 rnds even in dc.

**Inc rnd**: Work 2 dc in first sc, [dc one-quarter of the way around, 2 dc in next st] 3 times, dc in each st to end—4 sts increased.

Rep from * until cover is desired length when stretched.

### *all shades:*

**Next rnd**: Sc tbl in each st around.

**Next rnd**: Sc in each st around, join with a sl st in top of first sc. Fasten off.

### *finishing:*

Weave in all ends using a tapestry needle. Finish according to the instructions on page 101.

# nesting bowls

*These small bowls can contain just about anything, but I imagine them being used to hold keys, paper clips, rubber bands—whatever you need to add a bit of energy and brightness to your home office.*

## FINISHED MEASUREMENTS

X-Small: approximately 2¾ inches (7 cm) diameter and ¾ inches (2 cm) tall.

Small: approximately 3¾ inches (9.5 cm) diameter and 1¼ inches (3 cm) tall.

Medium: approximately 4¼ inches (11 cm) diameter and 1½ inches (4 cm) tall.

Large: approximately 4¾ inches (12 cm) diameter and 1¾ inches (4.5 cm) tall.

## MATERIALS

300 yards (274 meters) sport weight yarn (shown in Frabjous Fibers/Wonderland Yarns Mad Hatter, in gradient color Off With Her Red, 4 hanks)

Size F-5 (3.75 mm) crochet hook, or size needed to obtain gauge

Tapestry needle

## GAUGE

21 sts and 26 rnds = 4 inches (10 cm) in single crochet.

## NOTES

These baskets are worked in the round spirally, without joining at the end of each round.

## PATTERN

**Foundation ring**: Ch 3, join in the round with a sl st in first ch to form a ring.

**Rnd 1**: Work 10 sc around ring—10 sts.

**Rnd 2**: Work 2 sc in each st around—20 sts.

**Rnd 3**: Sc in each st around.

**Rnds 4 and 5**: Repeat rnds 2 and 3—40 sts.

**Rnd 6**: Sc in each st around. End size X-Small here.

**Rnd 7**: *Sc in next st, 2 sc in next st; repeat from * around—60 sts.

**Rnds 8 and 9**: Sc in each st around. End size Small after rnd 9.

**Rnd 10**: *Sc in next 2 sts, 2 sc in next st; repeat from * around—80 sts.

**Rnds 11 and 12**: Sc in each st around. End size Medium after rnd 12.

**Rnd 13**: *Sc in next 3 sts, 2 sc in next st; repeat from * around—100 sts.

**Rnds 14 and 15**: Sc in each st around. End size Large after rnd 15.

## *size x-small only:*

**Rnd 7**: *Sc in next 4 sts, 2 sc in next st; repeat from * around—48 sts.

Work 10 rnds even in sc, join with a sl st in top of next st at end of last rnd.

## *size small only:*

**Rnd 10**: *Sc in next 4 sts, 2 sc in next st; repeat from * around—72 sts.

Work 12 rnds even in sc, join with a sl st in top of next st at end of last rnd.

## *size medium only:*

**Rnd 13**: *Sc in next 4 sts, 2 sc in next st; repeat from * around—96 sts.

Work 14 rnds even in sc, join with a sl st in top of next st at end of last rnd.

## *size large only:*

**Rnd 16**: *Sc in next 4 sts, 2 sc in next st; repeat from * around—120 sts.

Work 16 rnds even in sc, join with a sl st in top of next st at end of last rnd.

## *all sizes:*

Insert hook into space between 2 sts 6 rows down from top edge and work 1 sl st, *insert hook into next st along top edge and into space between next 2 sts 6 rows down from top edge, yarn over and pull through all loops on hook; repeat from * around. Fasten off.

## *finishing:*

Weave in all ends using a tapestry needle.

# mason jar cover

*Candles are the quintessential Fire element, and as such are very powerful. Lighting a candle can uplift and expand the energy of your home—and that energy can go anywhere you need it most, from three green candles at the door to invite warmth, to eight blue candles in a left-hand corner of your home to spark inspiration.*

*The earthy orange pictured would be ideal for a library or living room, where it could promote peace and stimulate the intuition.*

## FINISHED MEASUREMENTS

3¼ inches (8.5 cm) diameter and 3½ inches (9 cm) high.

## MATERIALS

25 yards (23 meters) lace weight yarn (shown in Dragonfly Fibers Pixie, in color Hidalgo, 1 hank)

Size G-6 (4 mm) crochet hook, or size needed to obtain gauge

Tapestry needle

Safety pin

Mason jar

## GAUGE

16 sts and 8½ rnds = 4 inches (10 cm) in double crochet.

## NOTES

After working the first round, the bottom and sides are worked in spiral fashion without joining at the end of each round. A safety pin is used to mark the end of the round, and is moved up after each round.

## PATTERN

**Foundation ring**: Ch 3, join in the rnd with a slip st in first ch to form a ring, ch 1.

**Rnd 1**: Work 9 sc around ring, ch 1—9 sts.

**Rnd 2**: Dc in each st around, place safety pin in last st to mark end of rnd.

**Rnd 3**: Work 2 dc in each st around—18 sts.

**Rnd 4**: Repeat rnd 3—36 sts.

**Rnd 5**: Dc in next st, *ch 2, skip 2 sts, dc in next st; repeat from * to end of rnd, ending last repeat with dc in top of first st—13 dc and 12 ch-sp.

**Rnd 6**: *Ch 2, dc in ch-sp; repeat from * around—12 dc and 12 ch-sp.

**Rnds 7 and 8**: Repeat rnd 6.

**Rnd 9**: Repeat rnd 6, ch 2, join with a sl st in first ch-sp of rnd.

**Next rnd**: Sc in each st and 2 sc in each ch-sp around—36 sc.

**Next rnd**: *Sc in next st, skip 1 st; repeat from * around, join with a sl st in top of first sc—18 sts. Fasten off.

*finishing:*

Weave in all ends using a tapestry needle.

Slide over the mason jar—it'll be a tight fit.

# star blanket

*This airy afghan is shaped as an eight-pointed star, a symbol that has many meanings throughout the world. It's a sign of rebirth, of prosperity, and of chaos—all of which are certainly represented by Fire, as well.*

## FINISHED MEASUREMENTS

Approximately 58 inches (147.5 cm) diameter.

## MATERIALS

1,126 yards (1,029 meters) bulky weight yarn (shown in Plymouth Tuscan Aire, in color 03 Berry Heather, 7 balls)

Size I-9 (5.5 mm) crochet hook, or size needed to obtain gauge

Tapestry needle

## GAUGE

8 sts and 4 rnds = 4 inches (10 cm) in triple crochet.

## PATTERN

**Foundation ring**: Ch 5, join in the rnd with a sl st in first ch to form a ring.

**Rnd 1**: Ch 3 (counts as tr), work 15 tr around ring, join with a sl st in top of beginning ch—16 sts.

**Rnd 2**: Ch 3 (counts as tr), [tr, ch 3, 2 tr] in first st, *skip next st, [2 tr, ch 3, 2 tr] in next st; repeat from * around, join with a sl st in top of beginning ch—32 sts and 8 ch-sp.

**Rnd 3**: Ch 3 (counts as tr), skip 1 st, *[3 tr, ch 3, 3 tr] in next ch-3 sp, skip 1 st, tr in each st to 1 st before next ch-3 sp, skip 1 st; repeat from * around, join with a sl st in top of beginning ch—32 sts increased.

Repeat last rnd 14 times more, or until blanket has reached desired size. Fasten off.

### finishing:

Weave in all ends using a tapestry needle. Block as instructed on page 101.

# curtain ties

*As the element of Fire is the element of destruction as well as energy and renewal, it can be important to use it sparingly. A little goes a long way. But we should not do without it entirely, and the best way to bring its energy into your home is by inviting that most natural of all fires—the sun. Use these fiery curtain ties to pull back the shades and let in the light.*

## FINISHED MEASUREMENTS

2½ inches (6.5 cm) wide and 29 inches (73.5 cm) long, excluding fringe.

## MATERIALS

75 yards (68 meters) fingering weight yarn (shown in Dragonfly Yarns Pixie, in color Turning Leaves, 1 hank)

Size H-8 (5 mm) crochet hook, or size needed to obtain gauge

Tapestry needle

## GAUGE

19 sts and 7½ rows = 4 inches (10 cm) in cluster stitch.

### cluster

[Yarn over, insert hook, yarn over and draw through a loop] 3 times in same st (7 loops on hook), yarn over and draw through all 7 loops (1 loop remains on hook), ch 1.

## PATTERN

**Foundation ch**: Ch 12.

**Set-up row**: *Skip 2 ch, 2 clusters in next ch; repeat from * to end.

**Next row**: Ch 2, work 2 clusters in space between 2 clusters from previous row; repeat from * to end.

Repeat last row until piece measures 29 inches (73.5 cm), or longer if desired. Fasten off.

### finishing:

Weave in all ends using a tapestry needle.

Cut 32 pieces of yarn, each 8 inches (20.5 cm) long, for each tie. Holding 4 pieces of yarn together, use crochet hook to attach each fringe to center of each cluster at both ends of tie.

# EARTH

THE ELEMENT OF EARTH REPRESENTS STABILITY, FEELING GROUNDED. It is the base for all the other elements, and for your entire life, and every home should have plenty of Earth represented in it.

Contrary, perhaps, to our modern expectations, Earth's shape in Feng Shui is square, and flat—remember that the principles of Feng Shui date back for centuries! Its color is yellow, though it is equally brought to mind by earth tones like brown and sand. Pottery and other ceramics are a great way to ground your home in Earth, and a draft blocker, a floor pillow, or an area rug can help keep the energy of your home low to the ground, stable, and warm.

Earth nourishes two of the most important bagua centers in your home—your relationships with others, and your relationship with yourself. You can assist Earth by feeding it Fire, as ashes turn to dirt, which then turns to new growth. If you want to balance Earth, bring some Wood into your home, as Wood is that new growth, that stretching away from the ground.

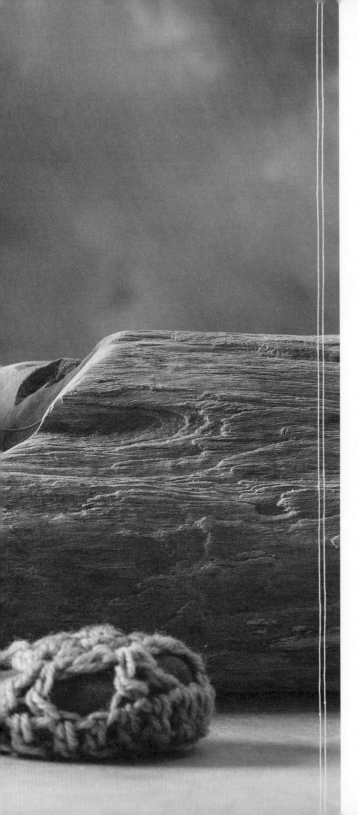

# covered stones

*When my husband saw these, he was skeptical. "We're making sweaters for rocks now?"*

*Yes. Yes, we are. Because rocks, those lowly bits of earth, are beautiful. We can bring our attention to that beauty by adding a touch of softness, of lace, of color—I learned that from Margaret Oomen's gorgeous, lacy crocheted rocks. These are much simpler, suitable for the beginning crocheter—but they, too, are works of art, meant to inspire us and ground us, both at the same time.*

## FINISHED MEASUREMENTS

Varies with size of stone.

## MATERIALS

25 yards (23 meters) fingering weight yarn for each cover (shown in Debbie Bliss Rialto 4-ply, in colors #22002 Cream and #22026 Mustard, 1 ball for each cover)

Size F-5 (3.75 mm) crochet hook, or size needed to obtain gauge (see Gauge note)

Tapestry needle

Smooth, rounded stones, between 2 and 4 inches (5 and 10 cm) in diameter

## GAUGE

28 sts and 28 rnds = 4 inches (10 cm) in single crochet.

Gauge is not critical for this pattern, though if your gauge is different, your finished measurements will not be the same.

## PATTERN

**Foundation ch**: Ch 6, join in the rnd with a sl st in first ch to form a ring.

**Rnd 1**: Ch 1, work 9 sc around ring, join with a sl st in beginning ch—10 sts.

**Rnd 2**: Ch 1, *sc in next st, ch 2, skip 1 st; repeat from * around, join with a sl st in beginning ch—5 sts and 5 ch-sp.

**Rnd 3**: Ch 1, dc in ch-2 sp, ch 2, *2 dc in next ch-2 sp, ch 2; repeat from * around, join with a sl st in beginning ch—10 sts and 5 ch-sp.

Hold piece over your stone. Does it just about cover the surface at the largest diameter? If so, skip ahead to Finishing. If not, keep going.

**Rnd 4**: Turn work, ch 1, 2 dc in ch-2 sp, ch 2, *3 dc in next ch-2 sp, ch 2; repeat from * around, join with a sl st in beginning ch—15 sts and 5 ch-sp.

Try the piece on your rock again. If it fits, skip ahead to Finishing. If not, carry on for one more round.

**Rnd 5**: Turn work, ch 1, 3 dc in ch-2 sp, ch 2, *4 dc in next ch-2 sp, ch 2; repeat from * around, join with a sl st in beginning ch—20 sts and 5 ch-sp.

*finishing:*

Weave in end from foundation ch using a tapestry needle.

**Next rnd**: Ch 1, dc in each st and ch around, join with a sl st to beginning ch.

**Next rnd**: [Sc2tog] around. Fasten off. *Note:* You may find that you need to insert the rock and work the last round around the rock, but usually that isn't necessary.

Weave in remaining end using a tapestry needle. Slip cover over the stone.

# floor cushion

*Sometimes, in order to connect to the earth, you need to get low. You need to sit on the ground or the floor and feel that sense of nourishment and stability. But ... sometimes the ground or the floor can be a bit uncomfortable.*

*There is no reason to have any kind of discomfort in your home, if you can avoid it. Make yourself a nice, thick floor cushion so that you can ground yourself, while still caring for yourself.*

## FINISHED MEASUREMENTS

15 inches (38 cm) wide by 17 inches (43 cm) long by 4 inches (10 cm) thick.

## MATERIALS

1,200 yards (1,097 meters) worsted weight yarn: 667 yards (610 meters) MC, 178 yards (163 meters) each CC1, CC2, and CC3 (shown in Berroco Vintage, in colors #5101 Mochi [MC], 3 hanks; #5192 Chana Dal [CC1], #5179 Chocolate [CC2], and #5105 Oats [CC3], 1 hank each)

Size F-5 (3.75 mm) crochet hook, or size needed to obtain gauge

Tapestry needle

15-inch (38 cm) by 17-inch (43 cm) by 4-inch (10 cm) foam cushion

## GAUGE

13½ sts and 16 rows = 4 inches (10 cm) in spike stitch crochet.

## spike stitch

Insert hook from front to back into st 2 rows below, yarn over and pull up a loop to height of current row, yarn over and pull through both loops on hook.

## PATTERN

### cushion (make 2):

**Foundation ch**: Using MC, ch 52.

**Row 1 (RS)**: Begin in 2nd ch from hook, sc in each ch across—51 sts.

**Row 2 (WS)**: Ch 1 and turn, sc in each st across.

**Rows 3 and 4**: Repeat row 2 twice more.

*Change to CC1.

*Note: For all color changes, drop yarn, but do not cut it. When it is time to change back to that color, simply lift it up alongside your work, taking care not to pull too tightly.*

**Spike row (RS)**: Ch 1, turn, sc in next 4 sts, [spike st in next st, sc in next 5 sts] to last 5 sts, spike st in next st, sc in each st to end.

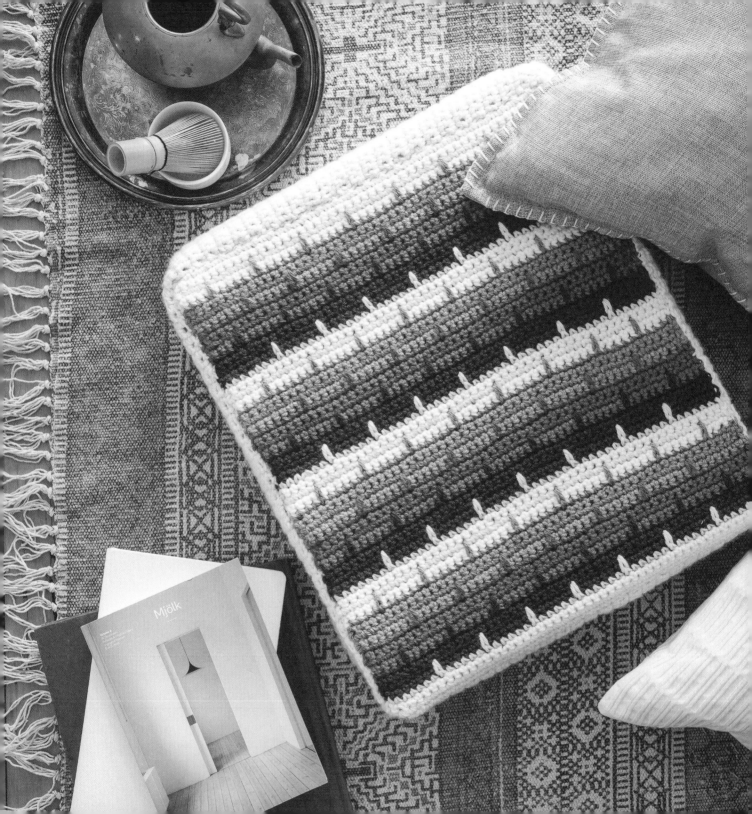

**Next 3 rows**: Ch 1 and turn, sc in each st across.

Change to CC2.

**Spike row (RS)**: Ch 1 and turn, sc in next 7 sts, [spike st in next st, sc in next 5 sts] to last 8 sts, spike st in next st, sc in each st to end.

**Next 3 rows**: Ch 1 and turn, sc in each st across.

Change to CC3.

**Spike row (RS)**: Ch 1 and turn, sc in next 4 sts, [spike st in next st, sc in next 5 sts] to last 5 sts, spike st in next st, sc in each st to end.

**Next 3 rows**: Ch 1 and turn, sc in each st across.

Change to MC.

**Spike row (RS)**: Ch 1 and turn, sc in next 7 sts, [spike st in next st, sc in next 5 sts] to last 8 sts, spike st in next st, sc in each st to end.

**Next 3 rows**: Ch 1 and turn, sc in each st across.

Repeat from * 3 times more.

## edging:

**Foundation ch**: Using MC, ch 17.

**Row 1**: Begin in 2nd ch from hook, sc in each ch across—16 sts.

**Row 2**: Ch 1 and turn, sc in each st across.

Repeat row 2 until piece measures 64 inches (162.5 cm) when stretched slightly. Fasten off.

## finishing:

Weave in all ends using a tapestry needle. Block all pieces as instructed on page 101.

Holding the bottom and edging pieces with RS together (WS facing out), use a tapestry needle to sew edging to cushion bottom, keeping strands of yarn at side away from seams as you sew, and with ends of edging meet at a corner. Sew beginning and ending edges together.

Holding the top and edging pieces with RS together, sew along 3 sides. Turn cushion with RS facing. Insert foam, then sew the remaining side closed.

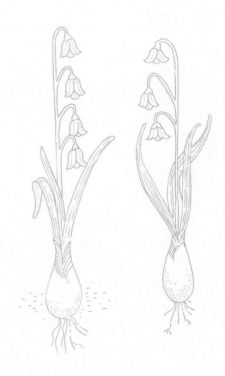

# scatter rug

*This cozy, squishy rug is perfect for curling up in front of the fire, though if you have a pet you'll probably have to fight them for it. You can use the suggested stripe pattern, or create something new—it's very simple, and very quick to work.*

## FINISHED MEASUREMENTS

34 inches (86.5 cm) diameter.

## MATERIALS

495 yards (452 meters) super bulky weight yarn: 255 yards (233 meters) MC, 240 yards (219 meters) CC (shown in Lion Brand Wool-Ease Thick & Quick, in color #640-123 Oatmeal [MC], 5 skeins; and #640-124 Barley [CC], 3 skeins)

Size K-10½ (6.5 mm) crochet hook, or size needed to obtain gauge

Tapestry needle

## GAUGE

8 sts and 4 rnds = 4 inches (10 cm) in double crochet.

## PATTERN

**Foundation ring**: Using MC, ch 4, join in the rnd with a sl st in first ch to form a ring.

**Rnd 1**: Ch 2 (counts as dc), work 11 dc around ring, join with a sl st in top of beginning ch—12 sts.

**Rnd 2**: Turn and ch 2 (counts as dc), dc in st at base of ch, work 2 dc in each st around, change to CC and join with a sl st in top of beginning ch—24 sts.

**Rnd 3**: Turn and ch 2 (counts as dc), dc in st at base of ch, *dc in next st, 2 dc in next st; repeat from * to last st, dc in next st, join with a sl st in top of beginning ch—36 sts.

**Rnd 4**: Turn and ch 2 (counts as dc), dc in st at base of ch, *dc in next 2 sts, 2 dc in next st; repeat from * to last 2 sts, dc in next 2 sts, join with a sl st in top of beginning ch—48 sts.

**Rnd 5**: Turn and ch 2 (counts as dc), dc in st at base of ch, *dc in next 3 sts, 2 dc in next st; repeat from * to last 3 sts, dc in next 3 sts, change to MC and join with a sl st in top of beginning ch—60 sts.

**Rnd 6**: Turn and ch 2 (counts as dc), dc in st at base of ch, *dc in next 4 sts, 2 dc in next st; repeat from * to last 4 sts, dc in next 4 sts, join with a sl st in top of beginning ch—72 sts.

**Rnd 7**: Turn and ch 2 (counts as dc), dc in st at base of ch, *dc in next 5 sts, 2 dc in next st; repeat from * to last 5 sts, dc in next 5 sts, join with a sl st in top of beginning ch—84 sts.

**Rnd 8**: Turn and ch 2 (counts as dc), dc in st at base of ch, *dc in next 6 sts, 2 dc in next st; repeat from * to last 6 sts, dc in next 6 sts, change to CC and join with a sl st in top of beginning ch—96 sts.

**Rnd 9**: Turn and ch 2 (counts as dc), dc in st at base of ch, *dc in next 7 sts, 2 dc in next st; repeat from * to last 7 sts, dc in next 7 sts, join with a sl st in top of beginning ch—108 sts.

**Rnd 10**: Turn and ch 2 (counts as dc), dc in st at base of ch, *dc in next 8 sts, 2 dc in next st; repeat from * to last 8 sts, dc in next 8 sts, join with a sl st in top of beginning ch—120 sts.

**Rnd 11**: Turn and ch 2 (counts as dc), dc in st at base of ch, *dc in next 9 sts, 2 dc in next st; repeat from * to last 9 sts, dc in next 9 sts, change to MC and join with a sl st in top of beginning ch—132 sts.

**Rnd 12**: Turn and ch 2 (counts as dc), dc in st at base of ch, *dc in next 10 sts, 2 dc in next st; repeat from * to last 10 sts, dc in next 10 sts, join with a sl st in top of beginning ch—144 sts.

**Rnd 13**: Turn and ch 2 (counts as dc), dc in st at base of ch, *dc in next 11 sts, 2 dc in next st; repeat from * to last 11 sts, dc in next 11 sts, join with a sl st in top of beginning ch—156 sts.

**Rnd 14**: Turn and ch 2 (counts as dc), dc in st at base of ch, *dc in next 12 sts, 2 dc in next st; repeat from * to last 12 sts, change to CC and join with a sl st in top of beginning ch—168 sts.

**Rnd 15**: Turn and ch 2 (counts as dc), dc in st at base of ch, *dc in next 13 sts, 2 dc in next st; repeat from * to last 13 sts, dc in next 13 sts, change to MC and join with a sl st in top of beginning ch—180 sts.

**Rnd 16**: Turn and ch 2 (counts as dc), dc in st at base of ch, *dc in next 14 sts, 2 dc in next st; repeat from * to last 14 sts, dc in next 14 sts, change to CC and join with a sl st in top of beginning ch—192 sts.

**Rnd 17**: Turn and ch 2 (counts as dc), dc in st at base of ch, *dc in next 15 sts, 2 dc in next st; repeat from * to last 15 sts, dc in next 15 sts, join with a sl st in top of beginning ch—204 sts. Fasten off.

*finishing:*

Weave in all ends using a tapestry needle. Block as instructed on page 101.

# afghan

*Inspired by the log cabin quilts made popular during the Great Depression, this afghan is worked in sections, each piece expanding upon what was just completed. The colors circle the blanket, and your eyes follow their pattern, much like the steps we walk in a meditation maze.*

## FINISHED MEASUREMENTS

Approximately 50½ inches (128.5 cm) wide by 52½ inches (133.5 cm) long.

## MATERIALS

1977 yards (1808 meters) bulky weight yarn: 635 yards (581 meters) MC, 647 yards (591 meters) CC1, and 695 yards (635 meters) CC2 (shown in Viking of Norway Cream, in colors #104 Cream [MC], 4 balls; #107 Sand [CC1], 4 balls; and #108 Brown [CC2], 5 balls)

Size H-8 (5 mm) crochet hook, or size needed to obtain gauge

Tapestry needle

## GAUGE

12 sts and 6 rows = 4 inches (10 cm) in double crochet.

## PATTERN

### center block:

**Foundation ch**: Using MC, ch 25.

**Row 1**: Begin in 2nd ch from hook and dc in each ch across—24 sts.

**Row 2**: Ch 2 and turn, dc tbl in each st across.

**Row 3**: Ch 1 and turn, dc in each st across.

Repeat rows 2 and 3 until piece measures 10 inches (25.5 cm). Fasten off.

### band 1:

**Row 1**: Rotate center block 90 degrees to the left, join CC1 and work 26 sc evenly spaced along side of block.

**Row 2**: Ch 2 and turn, dc in each st across.

**Rows 3–7**: Repeat row 2. Fasten off.

### band 2:

**Row 1**: Rotate piece 90 degrees to the left, join CC2 and work 23 sc along bottom of center block, then 15 sc along side of Band 1—38 sts.

**Rows 2–7**: Repeat rows 2–7 of Band 1. Fasten off.

## band 3:

**Row 1**: Rotate piece 90 degrees to the left, join MC and work 25 sc along side of center block, then 15 sc along side of Band 2—40 sts.

**Rows 2–7**: Repeat rows 2–7 of Band 1. Fasten off.

## band 4:

**Row 1**: Rotate piece 90 degrees to the left, join CC1 and work 15 sc along side of Band 1, 22 sc across remaining edge of center block, then 15 sc along side of Band 3—52 sts.

**Rows 2–7**: Repeat rows 2–7 of Band 1. Fasten off.

## band 5:

**Row 1**: Rotate piece 90 degrees to the left, join CC2 and work 15 sc along side of Band 2, 24 sc along top of Band 1, then 15 sc along side of Band 4—54 sts.

**Rows 2–7**: Repeat rows 2–7 of Band 1. Fasten off.

## band 6:

**Row 1**: Rotate piece 90 degrees to the left, join MC and work 15 sc along side of Band 3, 36 sts along top of Band 2, then 15 sc along side of Band 5—66 sts.

**Rows 2–7**: Repeat rows 2–7 of Band 1. Fasten off.

## band 7:

**Row 1**: Rotate piece 90 degrees to the left, join CC1 and work 15 sc along side of Band 4, 38 sc along top of Band 3, then 15 sc along side of Band 6—68 sts.

**Rows 2–7**: Repeat rows 2–7 of Band 1. Fasten off.

## band 8:

**Row 1**: Rotate piece 90 degrees to the left, join CC2 and work 15 sc along side of Band 5, 50 sc along top of Band 4, then 15 sc along side of Band 7—80 sts.

**Rows 2–7**: Repeat rows 2–7 of Band 1. Fasten off.

## band 9:

**Row 1**: Rotate piece 90 degrees to the left, join MC and work 15 sc along side of Band 6, 52 sc along top of Band 5, then 15 sc along side of Band 8—82 sts.

**Rows 2–7**: Repeat rows 2–7 of Band 1. Fasten off.

## band 10:

**Row 1**: Rotate piece 90 degrees to the left, join CC1 and work 15 sc along side of Band 7, 64 sc along top of Band 6, then 15 sc along side of Band 9—94 sts.

**Rows 2–7**: Repeat rows 2–7 of Band 1. Fasten off.

## band 11:

**Row 1**: Rotate piece 90 degrees to the left, join CC2 and work 15 sc along side of Band 8, 66 sc along top of Band 7, then 15 sc along side of Band 10—96 sts.

**Rows 2–7**: Repeat rows 2–7 of Band 1. Fasten off.

## band 12:

**Row 1**: Rotate piece 90 degrees to the left, join MC and work 15 sc along side of Band 9, 78 sc along top of Band 8, then 15 sc along side of Band 11—108 sts.

**Rows 2–7**: Repeat rows 2–7 of Band 1. Fasten off.

## band 13:

**Row 1**: Rotate piece 90 degrees to the left, join CC1 and work 15 sc along side of Band 10, 80 sc along top of Band 9, then 15 sc along side of Band 12—110 sts.

**Rows 2–7**: Repeat rows 2–7 of Band 1. Fasten off.

## band 14:

**Row 1**: Rotate piece 90 degrees to the left, join CC2 and work 15 sc along side of Band 11, 92 sc along top of Band 10, then 15 sc along side of Band 13—122 sts.

**Rows 2–7**: Repeat rows 2–7 of Band 1. Fasten off.

## band 15:

**Row 1**: Rotate piece 90 degrees to the left, join MC and work 15 sc along side of Band 12, 94 sc along top of Band 11, then 15 sc along side of Band 14—124 sts.

**Rows 2–7**: Repeat rows 2–7 of Band 1. Fasten off.

## band 16:

**Row 1**: Rotate piece 90 degrees to the left, join CC1 and work 15 sc along side of Band 13, 106 sc along top of Band 12, then 15 sc along side of Band 15—136 sts.

**Rows 2–7**: Repeat rows 2–7 of Band 1. Fasten off.

## band 17:

**Row 1**: Rotate piece 90 degrees to the left, join CC2 and work 15 sc along side of Band 14, 110 sc along top of Band 13, then 15 sc along side of Band 16—140 sts.

**Rows 2–7**: Repeat rows 2–7 of Band 1. Fasten off.

## band 18:

**Row 1**: Rotate piece 90 degrees to the left, join MC and work 15 sc along side of Band 15, 120 sc along top of Band 14, then 15 sc along side of Band 17—150 sts.

**Rows 2–7**: Repeat rows 2–7 of Band 1. Fasten off.

## band 19:

**Row 1**: Rotate piece 90 degrees to the left, join CC1 and work 15 sc along side of Band 16, 122 sc along top of Band 15, then 15 sc along side of Band 18—152 sts.

**Rows 2–7**: Repeat rows 2–7 of Band 1. Fasten off.

## band 20:

**Row 1**: Rotate piece 90 degrees to the left, join CC2 and work 15 sc along side of Band 17, 134 sc along top of Band 16, then 15 sc along side of Band 19—164 sts.

**Rows 2–7**: Repeat rows 2–7 of Band 1. Fasten off.

## finishing:

Weave in all ends using a tapestry needle. Block as instructed on page 101.

# tote

*This tote begs to be filled with things, from balls of yarn to dishtowels to dried flowers. Its nubby surface calls to mind the pebbled ground of the Northern Pacific coast, sand mixed with stones, hardening into sedimentary rock.*

## FINISHED MEASUREMENTS

32 inches (81.5 cm) top circumference and 8 inches (20.5 cm) tall.

## MATERIALS

300 yards (274 meters) bulky weight yarn (shown in Cascade Yarns Eco +, in color #4010 Straw, 1 hank)

Size F-5 (3.75 mm) crochet hook, or size needed to obtain gauge

Safety pin or locking stitch marker

Tapestry needle

## GAUGE

20 sts and 20 rnds = 4 inches (10 cm) in single crochet.

## NOTES

This tote is worked in the round spirally. Use a safety pin or locking stitch marker to indicate the end of each round, and move the marker up each round.

A smaller-than-usual crochet hook is used to create a firm fabric.

## PATTERN

*bottom:*

**Foundation ch**: Ch 13.

**Row 1**: Begin in 2nd ch from hook, sc in top loop of each ch across, rotate piece with opposite side of foundation ch at top and sc in bottom loop of each ch across—24 sts. Do not join.

**Rnd 1**: Work 2 sc in each of first 2 sts, sc in next 8 sts, 2 sc in each of next 4 sts, sc in next 8 sts, then 2 sc in each of last 2 sts—32 sts.

**Rnd 2**: Work 2 sc in each of next 3 sts, sc in next 10 sts, 2 sc in each of next 6 sts, sc in next 10 sts, then 2 sc in each of next 3 sts—44 sts.

**Rnd 3**: Sc in each st around.

**Rnd 4**: Work [2 sc in next st, sc in next st] 3 times, sc in next 10 sts, [2 sc in next st, sc in next st] 6 times, sc in next 10 sts, then [2 sc in next st, sc in next st] 3 times—56 sts.

**Rnd 5**: Sc in each st around.

**Rnd 6**: Work [2 sc in next st, sc in next st] 4 times, sc in next 12 sts, [2 sc in next st, sc in next st] 8 times, sc in each of next 12 sts, [2 sc in next st, sc in next st] 4 times—72 sts.

**Rnd 7**: Sc in each st around.

**Rnd 8**: Work [2 sc in next st, sc in next st] 7 times, sc in next 8 sts, [2 sc in next st, sc in next st] 14 times, sc in next 8 sts, [2 sc in next st, sc in next st] 7 times—100 sts.

## body:

*Work even in sc for 1 inch (2.5 cm).

**Increase rnd**: Sc around and increase 10 sts evenly spaced around.

Repeat from * 4 times more—150 sts.

Work even in sc for 1 inch (2.5 cm).

## handles:

**Rnd 1**: [Sc in next 50 sts, ch 20, skip next 25 sts] twice, join with a sl st in top of first st of rnd—140 sts remain.

**Rnd 2**: *Sc in next 8 sts, sc2tog; repeat from * around—126 sts remain.

**Rnd 3**: Sc in each st around.

**Rnd 4**: *Sc in next 7 sts, sc2tog; repeat from * around—112 sts remain.

**Rnd 5**: Sc in each st around, join with a sl st in in top of first st of rnd. Fasten off.

## finishing:

Weave in all ends using a tapestry needle.

# draft blocker

*While the sound of the wind whistling beneath your door can evoke mysterious stormy nights, the fact is that wind can be cold, and your heating bill doesn't much like it, either. This simple tube snugs right up at the foot of your door, blocks that wind, and keeps the warmth inside where it belongs.*

## FINISHED MEASUREMENTS

Approximately 37 inches (94 cm) long and 6¾ inches (17 cm) circumference.

## MATERIALS

150 yards (137 meters) Aran weight yarn (shown in Plymouth Homestead, in color #0019 Gold, 1 hank)

Size F-5 (3.75 mm) crochet hook, or size needed to obtain gauge

Tapestry needle

Approximately 3–3½ lbs (1.4–1.6 kg) of filler (shown using dried black beans, but any bean or lentil would work)

## GAUGE

18 sts and 17 rnds = 4 inches (10 cm) in single crochet.

## NOTES

This piece is worked in the round spirally without joining at the end of each round.

The weight of your filler will stretch the tube, so make sure to work fairly tightly.

## PATTERN

**Foundation ch**: Ch 30, join in the rnd with a sl st in first ch to form a ring.

**Rnd 1**: Ch 1, sc in each ch around. Do not join.

**Rnd 2**: Sc in each st around.

Repeat rnd 2 until piece measures 37 inches (94 cm) from beginning.

### *finishing:*

Holding tube flat, work sl st through both layers to join end. Fasten off. Weave in ends using a tapestry needle.

Fill tube with beans or lentils to desired firmness, making sure not to overfill. Use a tapestry needle to sew remaining end closed.

# METAL

METAL IS THE HARDEST OF ALL THE ELEMENTS. IT IS STRUCTURED, focused, and decisive. If you feel yourself flailing around in your life, if you have a hard time making choices and sticking to them, or if you have trouble following a schedule, it's probably a good idea to introduce more Metal into your surroundings.

As it happens, crocheting with metal is not only possible, but fun! You can make jewelry if you want to have some metal with you at all times, or you can make the napkin rings or small bowl from this chapter. You can also make items for your home that are traditionally made of or associated with metal, like the jewelry tray or picture frame. The shape of the Metal element is a circle, and its color is a shiny, non-reflective gray, and the throw pillow's circle that becomes a square is reminiscent of how yin and yang—in this case, Earth and Metal—work together to make a stable whole.

Metal is found in the Creativity and Offspring section, as well as the Friendship and Mentorship section of the bagua. It may seem counterintuitive to have creativity represented by structured Metal, rather than creative Wood, but this kind of creativity requires discipline and a careful plan—as, of course, does parenting. The friends in the Friendship and Mentorship section are of a very specific kind; these are the people whom we depend on, and who depend on us. Those relationships, too, require the kind of careful attention that Metal invokes.

Metal is nourished by Earth, since Earth, over time, compacts into Metal. If you want to support the Metal element in your home, add some Earth element, as well. But if you want to keep from being *too* structured, balance it with some Fire, which softens and melts Metal.

# bowl

*It's not often we get to craft with metal—usually that's left to the professionals! But crocheting with wire is deceptively simple. It feels a little awkward at first, since the wire doesn't flow through your fingers as yarn would, but there's something very satisfying about it.*

*This bowl will serve as a beautiful and unusual centerpiece, holding fresh fruit, beautiful rocks found on walks on the beach, dried flowers, pinecones—anything you like!*

## FINISHED MEASUREMENTS

Approximately 6 inches (15 cm) diameter and 3¼ inches (8.5 cm) tall.

## MATERIALS

30 yards (27 meters) 24-gauge artistic wire

Size F-5 (3.75 mm) hook (plastic or metal is best)

Wire cutters

Tapestry needle

## PATTERN

**Foundation ring**: Ch 4, join in the rnd with a sl st in first ch to form a ring.

**Rnd 1**: Ch 2 (counts as dc), work dc 11 around ring, join with a sl st in top of beginning ch—12 sts.

**Rnd 2**: Ch 2 (counts as dc), dc in same st as base of ch, *dc in next st, 2 dc in next st; repeat from * around, join with a sl st in top of beginning ch—18 sts.

**Rnd 3**: Ch 2 (counts as dc), dc in same st as base of ch, 2 dc in each st around, join with a sl st in top of beginning ch—36 sts.

**Rnd 4**: Ch 2 (counts as dc), dc in each st around, join with a sl st in top of beginning ch.

**Rnd 5**: Ch 2 (counts as dc), *2 dc in next st, dc in next st; repeat from * to last st, 2 dc in last st, join with a sl st in top of beginning ch—48 sts.

**Rnd 6**: Ch 2, dc in each st around, join with a sl st in top of beginning ch.

**Rnd 7**: Ch 2 (counts as dc), *2 dc in next st, dc in next st; repeat from * to last st, 2 dc in last st, join with a sl st in top of beginning ch—72 sts.

**Rnd 8**: Ch 2 (counts as dc), dc in each st around. Cut wire and fasten off.

## *finishing:*

Use tapestry needle to weave in all ends. Use wire cutters to trim ends close to bowl.

# napkin rings

*This is a very quick and easy project, but you can have a lot of fun with it. Your local craft store likely has a wide selection of beads, and you can incorporate them into your design in a way that appeals to you—small beads woven throughout, or just a couple of chunky ones, as shown.*

## FINISHED MEASUREMENTS

Approximately 1¾ inches (4.5 cm) diameter and 1¼ inches (3 cm) tall.

## MATERIALS

5 yards (4.6 meters) 24-gauge artistic wire for each napkin ring

Size F-5 (3.75 mm) crochet hook (plastic or metal is best)

Beads

Wire cutters

Tapestry needle

## NOTES

These napkin rings are worked in the round spirally without joining at the end of each round.

## PATTERN

String beads onto wire in desired order.

**Foundation ring**: Ch 18, join into rnd with a sl st in first ch to form a ring.

Work 2 rnds in sc.

**Next rnd**: Slide first bead up to hook, ch 1, letting bead rest within ch, [slide next bead up to hook and sc in next st] until all beads are attached, then sc to end of rnd. *Note:* For large beads, such as the ones pictured, lay bead flat against work and sc in st at opposite end of bead, skipping sts as needed, noting how many sts were skipped, and ch that number of sts above large bead on next rnd.

Work 2 more rnds in sc. Cut wire and fasten off.

## finishing:

Use tapestry needle to weave in all ends. Use wire cutters to trim ends close to napkin ring.

# cord cover

*There are so many things in our lives that are unavoidable—and they're often unsightly, too. And the reality is that we cannot avoid cords. Cords stick out from our lamps, from the wall where the cable for our internet comes in, from our chargers. We try not to notice them, but they are everywhere.*

*Cords feel so utilitarian to me, like metal—and indeed, if Metal is the element of focus, think about how cords literally focus energy.*

*Wrapping a cord with yarn not only makes it less unsightly, but also softens it, makes it a part of the home, not something to be shoved out of sight or glanced away from as quickly as possible. We live in a world of cords and electricity. Instead of resisting that, perhaps we should embrace it.*

## FINISHED MEASUREMENTS

Cord pictured is 5 feet (1.5 meters) long.

## MATERIALS

50 yards (46 meters) DK weight yarn (shown in Debbie Bliss Rialto DK, in color #33 Charcoal, 1 ball)

Size F-5 (3.75 mm) crochet hook, or size needed to obtain gauge (see Gauge note)

Tapestry needle

Cord for electronic device

## GAUGE

17 sts = 4 inches (10 cm) in single crochet.

Gauge is not critical for this pattern, though if your gauge is different, you may need extra yarn.

## PATTERN

Create a slip knot around your cord.

**Row 1**: *Insert hook into slip knot, yarn over and draw through a loop, stretching loop enough so that you can lift it over end of cord, remove hook and tighten loop, making sure it can slide along cord; repeat from * until cord is covered—approximately 5 sts for every 1 inch (3 cm); so if your cord is 12 inches (30.5 cm) long, you should chain on 60 sts. There should be enough stitches so that they can nestle next to each other without stretching, but not so many that the stitches are all bunched up.

**Row 2**: Turn work, insert hook between first 2 sts, yarn over and draw through a loop, *insert hook between next 2 sts, yarn over and draw through a loop (2 loops on hook), yarn over and draw through both loops on hook (1 loop remains); repeat from * to end of row. Fasten off.

## *finishing:*

Weave in all ends using a tapestry needle.

# jewelry tray

This little box is the marriage of something soft with something hard.

   The angles here are sharp (or as sharp as anything made out of yarn can be), and the bulky wool is held firm by the tight gauge, but remains soft enough to slouch just a bit. Toss in a few bracelets, necklaces, or earrings—anything you want to keep squared away, but held gently and with care.

## FINISHED MEASUREMENTS

4½ inches (11.5 cm) long by 4½ inches (11.5 cm) wide by 1½ inches (4 cm) tall.

## MATERIALS

65 yards (59 meters) Aran weight yarn (shown in Lion Brand Wool-Ease, in color #620-152 Oxford Grey, 1 skein)

Size G-6 (4 mm) crochet hook, or size needed to obtain gauge

Tapestry needle

## GAUGE

13 sts and 15 rows = 4 inches (10 cm) in single crochet.

## PATTERN

*bottom:*

**Foundation ch**: Ch 16.

**Row 1**: Begin in 2nd ch from hook, sc in each ch across—15 sts.

**Row 2**: Ch 1 and turn, sc in each st across.

Repeat row 2 until piece measures approximately 4½ inches (11.5 cm), or is roughly square. Fasten off.

*sides (make 4):*

**Foundation ch**: Ch 16.

Work 4 rows in sc same as bottom. Fasten off.

Holding pieces with WS together (RS is facing out), attach a long edge of each side to bottom using sl st through both layers. Sc ends of sides together at each corner.

Work 1 rnd of sl st around top edge. Fasten off.

*finishing:*

Weave in all ends using a tapestry needle.

# picture frame

*The curlicue edges of this picture frame mimic the ornate gilt frames found hanging on the walls in places like Versailles or Windsor Castle, but of course the fact that it is made out of yarn softens the effect, making it funky instead of fancy, offbeat instead of ostentatious.*

. . . . . . . . . . . . . . . . . . . . . . . . . . . . . . . . . . . . .

## FINISHED MEASUREMENTS

6¾ inches (17 cm) wide by 8½ inches (21.5 cm) tall; fits picture 4 inches (10 cm) by 6 inches (15 cm).

## MATERIALS

100 yards (91 meters) fingering weight yarn (shown in Dragonfly Fibers Pixie, in color Winter Woods, 1 hank)

Size E-4 (3.5 mm) crochet hook, or size needed to obtain gauge

Tapestry needle

Flexible cardboard, such as a cereal box

Scissors

Adhesive, such as craft glue or a hot glue gun

Picture-hanging strips

## GAUGE

27 sts = 4 inches (10 cm) in triple crochet.

## PATTERN

### *preparing the frame:*

Cut 2 cardboard rectangles, each 5 inches (12.5 cm) by 7 inches (18 cm). From one of the rectangles, cut out the center 4 inches (10 cm) by 6 inches (15 cm), leaving ½ inch (1.3 cm) border along each edge for the front of the frame. Discard the center portion. The remaining piece of cardboard is used for the back of the frame.

### *covering the frame:*

**Foundation ch**: Ch 163.

**Rnd 1**: Holding ch along inner edge of front of frame, work tr behind frame in 4th ch from hook, * work 3 tr in front of frame, tr behind frame; repeat from * around frame to end, join with a sl st in top of first tr—160 sts.

**Rnd 2**: *Sc in next 2 sts, sc2tog; repeat from * around—120 sts remain.

**Rnd 3**: *Sc in next st, skip 1 st, 5 dc in next st, skip 1 st; repeat from * around, join with a sl st in first st—180 sts. Fasten off.

### *inside edge:*

Attach yarn at inside edge, *sc in next 2 sts, sc2tog; repeat from * around, join with a sl st in first st. Fasten off.

### *finishing:*

Weave in all ends using a tapestry needle. Attach back of picture frame to front using adhesive, leaving top 5-inch (12.5 cm) edge open. Slide desired photograph into frame, and use picture-hanging strips to attach frame to wall.

# throw pillow

This pillow cover plays on the yin and yang of the Earth and Metal elements. A pillow is of course soft, while metal is the opposite. So how do you bring that mental sharpness, that streamlined thought that Metal represents, to something as gentle and comforting as a pillow . . . and, perhaps more importantly, why would you?

The how is simple enough. The metallic sheen and inflexibility of the linen yarn morphs from a circle into a square, marrying the two shapes that represent Earth and Metal. As for the why—bringing together the qualities of both of these elements harmonizes your environment, emphasizing each of their positive qualities while tempering the negative. Really, balancing the elements is what Feng Shui is all about.

## FINISHED MEASUREMENTS

19 inches (48.5 cm) square.

## MATERIALS

280 yards (256 meters) Aran weight linen yarn (shown in Rowan Pure Linen, in color #390 Gobi, 2 skeins)

Size G-6 (4 mm) crochet hook, or size needed to obtain gauge

Tapestry needle

19 inch (48 cm) by 19 inch (48 cm) pillow form

## GAUGE

10 sts and 3 rows = 4 inches (10 cm) in triple crochet.

## PATTERN

**Foundation ring**: Ch 4, join in the rnd with a sl st in first ch to form a ring.

**Rnd 1**: Ch 3 (counts as tr), work 15 tr around ring, join with a sl st in top of beginning ch—16 sts.

**Rnd 2**: Ch 3 (counts as tr), 3 tr in same st as ch, *ch 1, skip 1 st, work 4 tr in next st; repeat from * 6 times more, ch 1, skip last st, join with a sl st in top of beginning ch—32 sts and 8 ch-sp.

**Rnd 3**: Ch 4 (counts as tr, ch 1), *work 6 tr in next ch-1 sp, ch 1; repeat from * to last ch-1 sp, 5 tr in ch-1 sp, join with a sl st in 3rd ch of beginning ch—48 sts and 8 ch-sp.

**Rnd 4**: Ch 4 (counts as tr, ch 1), *[6 tr, ch 3, 6 tr] in next ch-1 sp, ch 1, 6 tr in next ch-1 sp, ch 1; repeat from * twice more, [6 tr, ch 3, 5 tr] in last ch-1 sp, join with a sl st in 3rd ch of beginning ch—72 sts and 12 ch-sp.

**Rnd 5**: Ch 3 (counts as tr), 5 tr in ch-1 sp, ch 1, *[6 tr, ch 3, 6 tr] in ch-3 sp, [ch 1, 6 tr in next ch-1 sp] twice; repeat from * twice more, [6 tr, ch 3, 6 tr] in ch-3 sp, ch 1, 6 tr in next ch-1 sp, ch 1, join with a sl st in top of beginning ch—96 sts and 16 ch-sp.

**Rnd 6**: Ch 4 (counts as tr, ch 1), 6 tr in ch-1 sp, ch 1, 6 tr in next ch-1 sp, ch 1, *[6 tr, ch 3, 6 tr] in ch-3 sp, [ch 1, 6 tr in next ch-1 sp] 3 times, ch 1; rep from * twice more, 6 tr in next ch-1 sp, ch 1, 5 tr in last ch-1 sp, join with a sl st in 3rd ch of beginning ch—120 sts and 20 ch-sp.

*Note: If your pillow is a smaller size than the pillow shown, skip to rnd 8.*

**Rnd 7**: Ch 3 (counts as tr), 5 tr in ch-1 sp, ch 1, 6 tr in next ch-1 sp, ch 1, *[6 tr, ch 3, 6 tr] in ch-3 sp, [ch 1, 6 tr in next ch-1 sp] 4 times, ch 1; repeat from * twice more, [6 tr, ch 3, 6 tr] in ch-3 sp, [ch 1, 6 tr in ch-1 sp] twice, ch 1, join with a sl st in top of beginning ch—144 sts and 24 ch-sp.

**Rnd 8**: Ch 2 (counts as dc), dc in each st and ch around, join with a sl st in top of beginning ch—176 sts. Fasten off.

Make second side same as first.

## *finishing:*

Weave in all ends using a tapestry needle. Block pieces as directed on page 101. Lay them against pillow—are they large enough to cover the pillow comfortably? If not, work another round or two (or more, as necessary) in dc until they fit. Make sure to work 3 dc in each corner st of every round. Block again if necessary.

Holding both pieces with WS together (RS is facing you), and working through both layers, sc along 3 edges. Slide pillow form inside and sc final edge closed. Weave in remaining ends using a tapestry needle.

# WATER

WATER IS THE MOST MYSTERIOUS OF ALL THE ELEMENTS. IT IS unstructured and unpredictable—it flows where it will, sometimes violently, or it can be still and glassy. But we need it to live, and so its energy represents sanctuary, healing, and spirituality. If you need a little more peace, a little more willingness to dwell in uncertainty, bring some of the Water element into your surroundings.

Mirrors and other reflective surfaces represent Water, as do dark colors and blues. Water doesn't have a specific shape attached to it, but anything sinuous and flowing will call it to mind. A dream catcher invokes the mysteries of Water, and the doilies flow in and out as you create them. Light, flowing curtains can ripple in the breeze, like a vertical river.

Water is made more powerful, more nourishing, by Metal, as both are reflective and reflecting. It is controlled by Earth, as the Earth guides it and gives it some structure, creating dams and falls.

# mirror cover

*Known as the "aspirin of Feng Shui," mirrors are pretty much a cure-all. They are amplifiers—think about how the mirror at the base of a microscope shines the light exactly where you need it to, and use a mirror in your home the same way. Mirrors attract and circulate energy, they bring light and movement into the home, and they reflect. That last one seems obvious, but it's not, really—it's important to see yourself and your surroundings from a different perspective.*

*These crocheted corners call attention to your mirror, highlighting its mysterious qualities while softening its hard edges.*

## FINISHED MEASUREMENTS

Each corner measures approximately 5½ inches (14 cm) wide at bottom edge and 4 inches (10 cm) tall.

## MATERIALS

154 yards (141 meters) sport weight yarn (shown in Madelinetosh Tosh Sport, in color Stargazing, 1 hank)

Size F-5 (3.75 mm) crochet hook, or size needed to obtain gauge

Tapestry needle

Square-edged mirror

Double-sided tape (optional)

## GAUGE

15 sts and 10 rows = 4 inches (10 cm) in double crochet.

## PATTERN

### front triangle (make 4):

**Foundation ch**: Ch 4.

**Row 1**: Begin in 2nd ch from hook, sc in each ch across—3 sts.

**Row 2**: Ch 2, 2 dc in first st, dc in each st to last st, 2 dc in last st—2 sts increased.

Repeat row 2 five times more—15 sts.

**Ruffle**: Ch 2, [2 tr, dc] in first st, *skip 1 st, [dc, 3 tr, dc] in next st; repeat from * to last 2 sts, skip 1 st, [dc, 2 tr] in last st—36 sts. Fasten off.

### back triangle (make 4):

**Foundation ch**: Ch 4.

**Row 1**: Begin in 2nd ch from hook, sc in each ch across—3 sts.

**Row 2**: Ch 2, 2 dc in first st, dc in each st to last st, 2 dc in last st—2 sts increased.

Repeat row 2 six times more—17 sts. Fasten off.

## joining:

Lay one front and one back triangle together with WS together (RS facing out). Working along the 2 short edges, work sc through both layers to form a pocket, leaving the ruffle side open. Repeat for remaining 3 pockets.

## attaching the corners:

**Top**: Measure pockets along one joined edge, stretching so the fabric is pulled taut. Multiply that number by 2, and subtract it from the width of your mirror. Attach yarn to one corner of first pocket and make a ch that measurement when stretched. Join the chain with a sl st to second corner. Before fastening off, check length by placing pockets on corresponding corners of mirror—if the chain is too short or too long, adjust the length of the chain. Fasten off when chain is the correct length. Repeat for bottom edge of the mirror.

**Sides**: Repeat for side edges.

## finishing:

Weave in all ends using a tapestry needle.

## placing on the mirror:

Stretch the corners onto the mirror. For a little extra security, use some double-sided tape to attach corners to the back of the mirror.

# dream catcher

*Traditionally, Native American dream catchers are quite tiny, and are given to infants upon birth. Each color and piece of the dream catcher is symbolic and sacred, as is the way it is made.*

*This is not a traditional dream catcher, but is instead a riff on the idea. Since the Water element is mysterious and full of the dark or light potential of dreams, an invocation of a dream catcher is both lovely and potentially useful.*

## FINISHED MEASUREMENTS

11¾ inches (30 cm) wide and 41 inches (104 cm) long.

## MATERIALS

100 yards (91 meters) fingering weight yarn (shown in Dragonfly Fibers Pixie, in color Kelpie, 1 hank)

30 yards (27 meters) narrow ribbon

Size E-4 (3.5 mm) crochet hook

Tapestry needle

Blocking pins (optional)

Blocking pad (optional)

12-inch diameter wooden hoop (the center of an embroidery hoop works well)

Scissors

Spare yarn

Craft flowers, beads, etc., as desired

Craft glue (optional)

## GAUGE

Gauge is not critical to this pattern.

## PATTERN

### center doily:

**Foundation ring:** Ch 6, join in the rnd with a sl st in first ch to form a ring.

**Rnd 1:** Ch 4 (counts as tr, ch 1), *tr in ring, ch 1; repeat from * 7 times more, join with a sl st in 3rd ch of beginning ch—9 sts and 9 ch-sp.

**Rnd 2:** Sc in next ch-sp, ch 3; repeat from * around, join with a sl st in base of first sc.

**Rnd 3:** Sl st to top of ch-3 sp, *ch 5, sc in next ch-3 sp; repeat from * 7 times more, ch 5, join with a sl st in base of beginning ch.

**Rnd 4:** Sl st to top of ch-5 sp, *ch 7, sc in next ch-5 sp; repeat from * 7 times more, ch 7, join with a sl st in base of beginning ch.

**Rnd 5:** Sl st to top of ch-7 sp, *ch 8, sc in next ch-7 sp; repeat from * 7 times more, ch 8, join with a sl st in base of beginning ch.

**Rnd 6**: Sl st to top of first ch-8 sp, *ch 9, sc in next ch-8 sp; repeat from * 7 times more, ch 9, join with a sl st in base of beginning ch.

**Rnd 7**: Sl st in first 4 ch, *sc in next ch, ch 3, skip 1 ch, sc in next ch, ch 6, sc in 5th ch of next loop; repeat from * 7 times more, sc in next ch, ch 3, skip 1 ch, sc in next ch, ch 6, join with sl st in base of first sc.

**Rnd 8**: Sc in 2nd ch of beginning ch, *ch 3, skip 1 ch, sc in next ch, ch 8, sc in first ch of next ch-3 sp; repeat from * 7 times more, ch 3, skip 1 ch, sc in next ch, ch 8, join with a sl st in base of first sc.

**Rnd 9**: *Ch 3, skip 1 ch, sc in next ch, ch 10, sc in first ch of next ch-3 sp; repeat from * 7 times more, ch 3, skip 1 ch, sc in next ch, ch 10, join with a sl st in base of beginning ch. Fasten off.

## finishing:

Weave in all ends using a tapestry needle. To emphasize the points, block doily following the directions on page 101. Then lay the doily flat on a blocking pad, or use a folded-up towel. Use the pins to stretch the points, moving them around as needed to make sure the points are stretched evenly.

## attaching the doily to the hoop:

Use the spare yarn to tie the doily to the hoop, sliding it around as necessary to make sure the center of the doily falls in the center of the hoop, and the points are evenly spaced. Thread your tapestry needle with whatever yarn or ribbon you choose and weave it through the loops and around the hoop, pulling and tying it tightly and securely. Trim ends.

## decorating:

Cut 15 pieces of ribbon or yarn, each approximately 60 inches/152.5 cm long. Loop ribbons or yarns along bottom of hoop as desired. You can tie beads in place, or glue craft flowers, feathers, or other items to the ribbons and to the center of the doily.

# mandala coasters

*Mandalas are sacred to a number of Eastern religions, and their history is long and varied. Essentially, though, a mandala is a tool used by spiritual practitioners to establish a sacred space, to find inner focus, and to aid in meditation.*

*Loosely translated from Sanskrit, the word "mandala" means "circle." It represents wholeness, a connection between each of us and the cosmic infinite. Some of these mandalas are harder than others, and so require a bit more concentration, which can be more or less meditative, depending on how long you've been crocheting. The first one is the easiest, and the last is the hardest. Whichever you choose, the act of making these mandalas can bring you deep into meditation, and the best part is, anytime you see them or use them, you can remember and go back to that peaceful state.*

## FINISHED MEASUREMENTS

Approximately 3½ inches (9 cm) diameter.

## MATERIALS

75 yards (68 meters) worsted weight yarn (shown in Rowan Softknit Cotton, in colors #585 Indigo Blue [MC], #584 Walnut [CC1], #573 China [CC2], and #587 Willow [CC3], 1 ball each)

Size F-5 (3.75 mm) crochet hook, or size needed to obtain gauge

Tapestry needle

## GAUGE

25 sts and 25 rows = 4 inches (10 cm) in single crochet.

## NOTES

For the first and second mandalas, the main color is used for more than one round, and for the fourth mandala, contrast color 2 is used for more than one round. When changing from that color to the next in the sequence, drop the yarn to the back of your work and carry it loosely up the back until it's needed again. Cut that yarn only when instructed.

## FIRST MANDALA

**Foundation ring**: Using MC, ch 3, join in the rnd with a sl st in first ch to form a ring.

**Rnd 1**: Work 8 sc around ring—8 sts.

**Rnd 2**: [Ch 3, sc] in first 7 sts, ch 3, join with a sl st in first ch of beginning ch—8 sts and 8 ch-sp.

**Rnd 3**: Change to CC1, ch 1, sc in each st and 2 sc in each ch-sp around, join with a sl st in top of first st—36 sts. Cut yarn.

**Rnd 4**: Change to MC, ch 1, sc in each st around, join with a sl st in top of first st.

**Rnd 5**: Change to CC2, ch 1, 2 sc in first st, sc in next st, *2 sc in next st, sc in next st; repeat from * around, join with a sl st in top of first st—54 sts. Cut yarn.

**Rnd 6**: Change to MC, ch 1, sc in each st around, join with a sl st in top of first st. Cut yarn.

**Rnd 7**: Change to CC3, ch 1, sc in each st around, join with a sl st in top of first st. Fasten off.

## SECOND MANDALA

**Foundation ring**: Using MC, ch 3, join in the rnd with a sl st in first ch to form a ring.

**Rnd 1**: Work 8 sc around ring—8 sts.

**Rnd 2**: Change to CC1, ch 1, 3 sc in each st around, join with a sl st in top of first st—24 sts. Cut yarn.

**Rnd 3**: Change to CC2, ch 2 (counts as dc), dc in next st, ch 1, skip 1 st, *dc in next 2 sts, ch 1, skip 1 st; repeat from * to end, join with a sl st in top of beginning ch—16 sts and 8 ch-sp. Cut yarn.

**Rnd 4**: Change to MC, ch 1, *5 dc in ch-1 sp; repeat from * around, join with a sl st in top of first dc—40 sts. Cut yarn.

**Rnd 5**: Change to CC3, ch 2 and turn, *5 dc in space between 2 dc clusters; repeat from * around, join with a sl st in top of beginning ch. Fasten off.

## THIRD MANDALA

**Foundation ring**: Using MC, ch 3, join in the rnd with a sl st in first ch to form a ring.

**Set-up rnd**: Work 8 sc around ring—8 sts.

*slice 1:*

**Row 1 (RS)**: 3 sc in next st, ch 1 and turn.

**Row 2 (WS)**: Sc in first st, 2 sc in next st, sc in next st, ch 2 and turn—4 sts.

**Row 3**: Dc in first st, ch 1, skip 2 sts, dc in next st, ch 2 and turn.

**Row 4**: Work 5 dc in ch-sp—5 sts. Fasten off, leaving a tail 6 inches (15 cm) long.

*slice 2:*

**Row 1 (RS)**: Join CC1 to next st of set-up rnd, work 3 sc in this st, ch 1 and turn.

**Rows 2–4**: Work same as Slice 1.

*slices 3–8:*

Repeat Slice 2, alternating colors as follows: CC2, CC3, MC, CC1, CC2, then CC3.

The mandala will look like a flower with loose petals and a lot of tails. Use tails to sew petals together along side edges.

**Next rnd**: Using MC, sc in each st around top edge—40 sts.

**Next rnd**: [Sc, ch 1] in each st around—40 sts and 40 ch-sp. Fasten off.

## FOURTH MANDALA

**Foundation ring**: Using CC2, ch 3, join in the rnd with a sl st in first ch to form a ring.

**Rnd 1**: Work 8 sc around ring—8 sts.

**Rnd 2**: Ch 1, work 3 sc in each st around—24 sts.

**Rnd 3**: Change to CC1, ch 2 (counts as dc), ch 1, skip 1 st, *dc in next st, ch 1, skip 1 st; repeat from * around, join with a sl st in top of first dc. Cut yarn.

**Rnd 4**: Change to CC2, ch 2 (counts as dc), 2 dc in next ch-sp, work 3 dc in each ch-sp around, join with a sl st in top of first dc—36 sts. Cut yarn.

**Rnd 5**: Change to CC3, ch 3 (counts as dc, ch 1), skip first st, *dc in next 2 sts, ch 1, skip 1 st; repeat from * around to last st, dc in next st, join with a sl st in top of beginning ch. Cut yarn.

*overlay:*

*Note: It may make your work easier if you use 3 pieces of contrasting yarn to mark equally spaced spokes from edge to edge.*

Change to MC, sc in same st, rotate work so that you're crocheting toward center of mandala, *work 3 sl sts down to bottom of rnd 4, ch 2 to skip over rnd 3, work 3 sl sts along rnds 2 and 1 to center. Rotate work to crochet back to outer edge, work at a slight angle and work 2 sl sts to top of rnd 2, ch 2 to skip over rnd 3, work 3 slip sts in rnds 4 and 5 to top edge, rotate work to crochet along top edge, work 3 sc along top edge; repeat from * 5 times more, join with a sl st in first sl st. Fasten off.

*finishing:*

Weave in all ends using a tapestry needle. Soak your mandalas in lukewarm water for five minutes or so, then lay flat to dry.

# doilies

*For most of us, doilies call to mind lukewarm tea and hope chests and musty-smelling furniture. But when you really look at them, they are lovely. They are refined, exquisite, and useful, as well.*

*Traditionally, of course, they are white and worked using thin thread and very tiny hooks. These more modern doilies are inspired by vintage patterns, but they are worked at a much larger gauge. The stitches ebb and flow like the gentle lapping of a lake, and bring forth that same serene coolness.*

## FINISHED MEASUREMENTS

Approximate diameters: Rising Sun Doily, 9 inches (23 cm); Evening Star Doily, 6½ inches (16.5 cm); Nosegay Doily, 6½ inches (16.5 cm); Jewel Doily, 8½ inches (21.5 cm); and Spiderweb Doily, 8¼ inches (21 cm).

## MATERIALS

50 yards (46 meters) fingering weight yarn for each doily (shown in various yarns, 1 hank/ball each: Malabrigo Mechita in color Pegaso [A]; Knit Picks Palette, in color Blue Note Heather [B]; Dragonfly Fibers Pixie, in color Mermaid [C]; Dragonfly Fibers Pixie, in color Kelpie [D]; and reclaimed cashmere yarn, in color light blue [E])

Size E-4 (3.5 mm) crochet hook

Tapestry needle

Blocking pins (optional)

Blocking pad (optional)

## GAUGE

Gauge is not critical to this pattern.

## NOTES

These doilies may be made using heavier yarn, though if you substitute a heavier yarn, they will be larger, and you may need more yarn to complete them.

## RISING SUN DOILY

**Foundation ring**: With A, ch 10, join in the rnd with a sl st in first ch to form a ring.

**Rnd 1**: Ch 5 (counts as dc, ch 2), [dc in ring, ch 2] 9 times, join with a sl st in 3rd ch of beginning ch—10 sts and 10 ch-sp.

**Rnd 2**: Sl st in next ch-sp, ch 3 (counts as dc), 2 dc in same ch-sp, *ch 2, 3 dc in next ch-2 sp; repeat from * around, ch 2, join with a sl st in top of beginning ch—30 sts and 10 ch-sp.

**Rnd 3**: Sl st to center dc of dc-cluster, *ch 5, sc in next ch-2 sp, ch 5, skip 1 dc, sc in next dc; repeat from * around, ending last repeat with sc in base of beginning ch—20 sts and 20 ch-sp.

**Rnd 4**: Sl st to center of first ch-sp, sc in same ch-sp, *ch 5, sc in next ch-sp; repeat from * around, ending last rep with sc in sl st before first sc.

**Rnd 5**: Sl st in first 2 ch, ch 4 (counts as tr), 2 tr in same ch-sp, *ch 2, 3 tr in next ch-sp; repeat from * around, ch 2, join with a sl st in top of beginning ch—60 sts and 20 ch-sp.

**Rnd 6**: Sl st in first tr, *ch 5, sc in next tr, ch 5, skip 1 tr, sc in next ch-sp; repeat from * around, ch 5, join with a sl st in first sl st. Fasten off.

## EVENING STAR DOILY

**Foundation ring**: With B, ch 5, join in the rnd with a sl st in first ch to form a ring.

**Rnd 1**: Ch 2 (counts as dc), work 9 dc around ring, join with a sl st in top of beginning ch—10 sts.

**Rnd 2**: Ch 5 (counts as tr, ch 2), *tr in next st, ch 2; repeat from * around, join with a sl st in 3rd ch of beginning ch—10 sts and 10 ch-sp.

**Rnd 3**: Sl st in ch-sp, ch 3 (counts as tr), 2 tr in same ch-2 sp, *ch 3, 3 tr in next ch-2 sp; repeat from * around, join with a sl st in top of beginning ch—30 sts and 10 ch-sp.

**Rnd 4**: Sl st to center tr of first tr-cluster, ch 3 (counts as tr), *[tr, dc, hdc, sc, hdc, dc, tr] in ch-3 sp, skip 1 tr, tr in next tr, skip next tr; repeat from * 8 times more, [tr, dc, hdc, sc, hdc, dc, tr] in next ch-3 sp, skip 1 tr, then join with a sl st in top of beginning ch—80 sts.

**Rnd 5**: Ch 6 (counts as sc, ch 5), skip first 4 sts, *sc in sc, ch 5, skip next 3 sts, sc in tr, ch 5, skip next 3 sts; repeat from * 8 times more, sc in sc, ch 5, skip next 3 sts, join with a sl st in base of of beginning ch. Fasten off.

## NOSEGAY DOILY

**Foundation ring**: With C, ch 10, join in the rnd with a sl st in first ch to form a ring.

**Rnd 1**: Ch 7 (counts as dc, ch 4), [dc in ring, ch 4] 6 times, join with a sl st in 3rd ch of beginning ch—7 sts and 7 ch-sp.

**Rnd 2**: [Sc, hdc, 5 dc, hdc, sc] in each ch-4 sp around, join with a sl st in base of first sc—63 sts.

**Rnd 3**: Turn work, ch 11 (counts as ch 7, tr), skip next 9 sts, tr between sts, *ch 7, skip next 9 sts, tr between sts; repeat from * 4 times more, join with a sl st in 4th ch of beginning ch—7 sts and 7 ch-sp.

**Rnd 4**: Ch 1, *work 9 sc in ch-sp, sc in next tr; repeat from * 5 times more, 9 sc in next ch-sp, join with a sl st in base of beginning ch—70 sts.

**Rnd 5**: [Sc, hdc, 2 dc, 4 tr, 2 dc, hdc, sc] in each ch-sp around, join with a sl st in base of first sc—84 sts. Fasten off.

## JEWEL DOILY

**Foundation ring**: With D, ch 8, join in the rnd with a sl st in first ch to form a ring.

**Rnd 1**: Ch 2 (counts as dc), work 11 dc around ring, join with a sl st to top of beginning ch—12 sts.

**Rnd 2**: Ch 3 (counts as dc), dc in same place, *dc in next st, 2 dc in next st; repeat from * to last st, dc in last st, join with a sl st in top of beginning ch—18 sts.

**Rnd 3**: Ch 7 (counts as dc, ch 4), *skip 2 sts, dc in next st, ch 4; repeat from * around, join with a sl st in 3rd ch of beginning ch—6 sts and 6 ch-sp.

**Rnd 4**: [Sl st, ch 3 (counts as dc), 2 dc, ch 3, 3 dc] in first ch-sp, [3 dc, ch 3, 3 dc] in each ch-sp around, join with a sl st top of beginning ch—36 sts and 6 ch-cp.

**Rnd 5**: Sl st to ch-3 sp, [ch 3 (counts as dc), 2 dc, ch 3, 3 dc] in ch-3 sp, ch 1, *[3 dc, ch 3, 3 dc] in next ch-3 sp, ch 1; repeat from * around, join with a sl st in top of beginning ch—36 sts and 12 ch-sp.

**Rnd 6**: Sl st to ch-3 sp, [ch 2 (counts as dc), 2 dc, ch 3, 3 dc] in ch-3 sp, ch 3, *[3 dc, ch 3, 3 dc] in next ch-3 sp, ch 3; repeat from * around, join with a sl st in top of beginning ch.

**Rnd 7**: Sl st to ch-3 sp, [ch 2 (counts as dc), 2 dc, ch 3, 3 dc] in ch-3 sp, ch 5, *[3 dc, ch 3, 3 dc] in next ch-3 sp, ch 5; repeat from * around, join with a sl st in top of beginning ch.

**Rnd 8**: Sl st to ch-3 sp, [ch 2 (counts as dc), 2 dc, ch 3, 3 dc] in ch-3 sp, ch 7, *[3 dc, ch 3, 3 dc] in next ch-3 sp, ch 7; rep from * around, join with a sl st in top of beginning ch. Fasten off.

## SPIDERWEB DOILY

**Foundation ring**: With E, ch 10, join in the rnd with a sl st in first ch to form a ring.

**Rnd 1**: Ch 2 (counts as hdc), work 13 hdc around ring, join with sl st in top of beginning ch—14 sts.

**Rnd 2**: Ch 4 (counts as dc, ch 1), *dc in next hdc, ch 1; repeat from * around, join with a sl st in 3rd ch of beginning ch—14 sts and 14 ch-sp.

**Rnd 3**: Sl st to next ch-sp, sc in same ch-sp, *ch 3, sc in next ch-sp; repeat from * around, join with a sl st in base of first sc.

**Rnd 4**: Sl st to center of next ch-sp, sc in same ch-sp, *ch 4, sc in next ch-sp; repeat from * around, join with a sl st in base of first sc.

**Rnd 5**: Sl st to center of next ch-sp, sc in same ch-sp, *ch 6, sc in next ch-sp; repeat from * around, join with a sl st in base of first sc.

**Rnd 6**: Sl st to center of next ch-sp, sc in same ch-sp, *ch 8, sc in next ch-sp; repeat from * around, join with a sl st in base of first sc.

**Rnd 7**: Sl st to center of next ch-sp, sc in same ch-sp, *ch 10, sc in next ch-sp; repeat from * around, join with a sl st in base of first sc. Fasten off.

### *finishing:*

Weave in all ends using a tapestry needle. Finish as directed on page 101. For the Jewel and Nosegay doilies, to emphasize the points, follow the directions on page 101. Then lay the doily flat on a blocking pad, or use a folded-up towel. Use the pins to stretch the points, moving them around as needed to make sure the points are stretched evenly.

# curtain

*Anything sinuous, mysterious, and dark brings to mind the Water element of Feng Shui. But at the same time, it's hard to imagine a blackout curtain being at all beneficial to anything about your home, unless it's to keep your bedroom dark. To compromise, this wavy blue curtain blocks some of the light, introducing just a bit of mystery and regeneration.*

## FINISHED MEASUREMENTS

Approximately 23 inches (58.5 cm) wide by 33 inches (84 cm) long.

## MATERIALS

610 yards (558 meters) fingering weight yarn (shown in Malabrigo Mechita, in color #MTA892 Pegaso, 2 hanks)

Size H-8 (5 mm) crochet hook, or size needed to obtain gauge

Tapestry needle

## GAUGE

16 sts and 7 rows = 4 inches (10 cm) in dc-cluster st.

## PATTERN

**Foundation ch**: Ch the desired width of your curtain, checking your st count to make sure it's a multiple of 6, plus 8 (curtain shown uses 80 sts).

**Set-up row**: Dc in 2nd ch from hook, *skip 2 ch, 3 dc in next ch; rep from * to last 3 sts, skip 2 ch, dc in last ch, ch 3 and turn.

**Row 1**: *3 dc between dc-cluster; rep from * to last st, 2 dc in top of turning ch, ch 3 and turn.

Repeat row 1 until piece is 4 inches (10 cm) less than desired length of curtain (curtain shown measures 29 inches [73.5 cm] long).

**Next row**: Ch 1, sc in each st across.

Repeat last row for 2 inches (5 cm).

Fold sc section in half, with last row worked at bottom of sc.

**Joining row**: Working through both layers, work 1 row of sc across. Fasten off.

## *edging:*

**Set-up row**: Attach yarn at bottom right edge of foundation ch, sc in each ch across, ch 3 and turn.

**Row 1**: Tr in each st across, turn.

**Row 2**: Ch 3 (counts as tr), [tr, ch 5, sl st in 5th ch from hook, tr, ch 3, sl st] in next st, *sc in next 2 sts, [sc, ch 3, tr, ch 5, sl st in 5th ch from hook, tr, ch 3, sl st] in next st; rep from * across. Fasten off.

## *finishing:*

Weave in all ends using a tapestry needle.

# hanging basket

*This basket can hang on a hook or on a doorknob, and it can hold everything from dishtowels to dried flowers to balls of yarn. More than anything, it looks like a really useful waterfall—which, to me, is the best way to invite the principles of Feng Shui into your home. It calls to mind the element of Water, but it serves a genuine purpose—and looks great, to boot.*

## FINISHED MEASUREMENTS

33 inches (84 cm) circumference at widest spot.

## MATERIALS

177 yards (162 meters) Aran weight yarn (shown in Tahki Aruba, in color #12 Midnight Sky, 2 balls)

Size H-8 (5 mm) crochet hook, or size needed to obtain gauge

Tapestry needle

Safety pins

## GAUGE

16 sts and 18 rnds = 4 inches (10 cm) in single crochet.

## NOTES

This basket is worked in the round spirally, without joining at the end of each round.

## PATTERN

**Foundation ring**: Ch 3, join in the rnd with a sl st in first ch to form a ring.

**Rnd 1**: Work 9 sc around ring—9 sts.

**Rnd 2**: Work 2 sc in each st around—18 sts.

**Rnd 3**: Sc in each st around.

**Rnd 4**: Work 2 sc in each st around—36 sts.

**Rnd 5**: Sc in each st around.

**Rnd 6**: *Sc in next st, 2 sc in next st; repeat from * around—54 sts.

**Rnds 7 and 8**: Sc in each st around.

**Rnd 9**: *Sc in next 2 sts, 2 sc in next st; repeat from * around—72 sts.

**Rnds 10 and 11**: Sc in each st around.

**Rnd 12**: *Sc in next 3 sts, 2 sc in next st; repeat from * around—90 sts.

**Rnds 13 and 14**: Sc in each st around.

**Rnd 15**: *Sc in next 4 sts, 2 sc in next st; repeat from * around—108 sts.

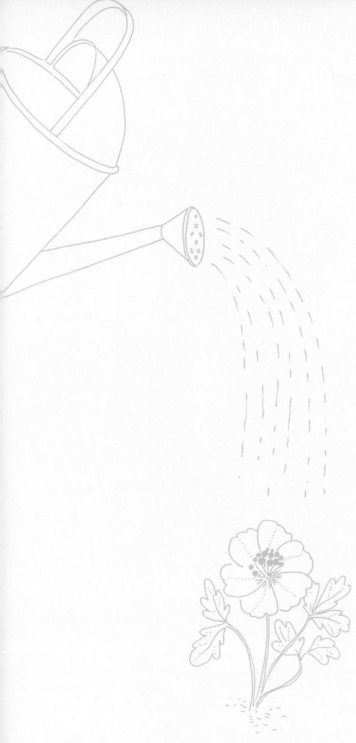

**Rnd 16**: [2 sc in next st, sc in next 35 sts, place safety pin] twice, 2 sc in next st, sc in remaining 35 sts—111 sts.

**Rnd 17**: [2 sc in next st, sc in each st to safety pin] twice, 2 sc in next st, sc in each st to end of rnd—3 sts increased.

**Rnds 18–24**: Repeat rnd 17 seven times more—135 sts.

**Rnd 25**: Sc in next st, [sc2tog] to end—68 sts.

**Rnd 26**: 2 sc in next st, sc in each st around—69 sts.

**Rnd 27**: 2 sc in next st, sc in next 46 sts, ch 1 and turn, sc in next 23 sts, ch 1 and turn, sc in next 21 sts, sc3tog, sc to end—68 sts.

**Rnd 28**: 2 sc in next st, sc in next 21 sts, sc3tog, sc in each st to end—67 sts.

**Rnd 29**: 2 sc in next st, sc in each st to end—68 sts.

## handle:

**Row 1**: Sc in next 6 sts, turn.

**Row 2**: Ch 1, sc in next 3 sts, turn.

Repeat row 2 until handle measures 4 inches (10 cm).

Fold handle over and join to edge of basket 6 sts from base of handle by working 3 sl sts through both layers. Fasten off.

## finishing:

Weave in all ends using a tapestry needle.

# ABBREVIATIONS

**beginning ch**
*beginning chain*

**CC**
*contrast color*

**ch**
*chain*

**ch-sp**
*chain-space*

**cm**
*centimeter(s)*

**dc**
*double crochet*

**dc2tog**
*double crochet 2 together
(1 stitch decreased)*

**dc3tog**
*double crochet 3 together
(2 stitches decreased)*

**hdc**
*half double crochet*

**kg**
*kilogram(s)*

**lb(s)**
*pound(s)*

**MC**
*main color*

**mm**
*millimeter(s)*

**rnd(s)**
*round(s)*

**RS**
*right side(s)*

**sc**
*single crochet*

**sc2tog**
*single crochet 2 together
(1 stitch decreased)*

**sl st**
*slip stitch*

**st(s)**
*stitch(es)*

**tbl**
*through back loop(s)*

**tr**
*triple/treble crochet*

**WS**
*wrong side(s)*

# STITCH GLOSSARY

**Chain (ch)**: Yarn over and draw a loop through the loop on your hook.

**Double crochet (dc)**: Yarn over (2 loops on hook), insert hook into next stitch, yarn over and draw through a loop (3 loops on hook), yarn over and draw through first 2 loops on hook (2 loops on hook), yarn over and draw yarn through remaining 2 loops on hook (1 loop remains on hook).

**Double crochet two together (dc2tog)**: [Yarn over, insert hook into next stitch, yarn over and draw through a loop] twice (5 loops on hook), yarn over and draw loop through all loops on hook (1 loop remains on hook).

**Double crochet three together (dc3tog)**: Work same as above, working into one more stitch (7 loops on hook before final yarn over and draw loop through all loops).

**Half double crochet (hdc)**: Yarn over (2 loops on hook), insert hook into next stitch, yarn over and draw through a loop (3 loops on hook), yarn over and draw through all loops on hook (1 loop remains on hook).

**Single crochet (sc)**: Insert hook into next stitch, yarn over and draw through a loop (2 loops on hook), yarn over and draw loop through both loops on hook (1 loop remains on hook).

**Single crochet two together (sc2tog)**: [Insert hook into next stitch, yarn over and draw through a loop] twice (3 loops on hook), yarn over and draw through all loops on hook (1 loop remains on hook).

**Slip stitch (sl st)**: Insert hook into next stitch, yarn over and pull loop to front and through loop on hook (1 loop on hook).

**Triple/treble crochet (tr)**: [Yarn over] twice (3 loops on hook), insert hook into next stitch, yarn over and draw through a loop (4 loops on hook), [yarn over and draw loop through first 2 loops on hook] 3 times (1 loop remains on hook).

# FINISHING

Several crocheted items can be deemed "complete" without this final step. Covered stones, stacking baskets, a mason jar cover—none of these need this extra bit of care and attention to make them look right. But frequently things like doilies, curtains, and table runners look lumpy and twisted unless they are blocked—that is, made wet and reshaped and dried.

You start by introducing moisture to the fabric. You can go slowly, with a steamer or a spray bottle, but honestly, if you're going to go to the trouble of blocking something, you should give yourself all the moisture you need to get it right, even if that means it'll take a while longer to dry. So just dunk the whole thing in a sink full of lukewarm water and let it soak for a few minutes.

Take it out and squeeze it gently to remove as much excess water as you can—but don't wring it—and then lay it flat to dry. Use your hands to arrange it into the shape you want. This is more challenging than it sounds, so be patient. You'll find that you need to adjust and readjust as you go, until all the stitches and edges are even.

Let it dry completely.

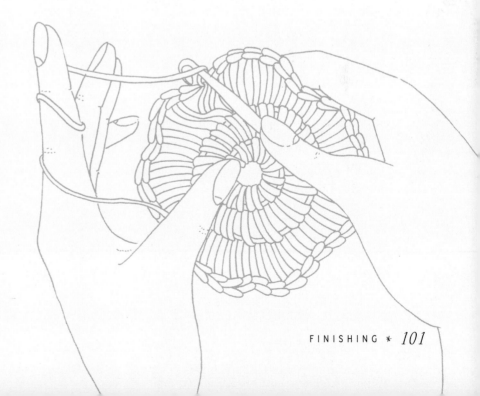

# ACKNOWLEDGMENTS

This project is incredibly unlikely since (full disclosure) like many knitters, I've always sort of disdained crochet. I was completely wrong.

Thank you to my mom, for teaching me. Thank you to Shannon Connors, for being someone I always knew could crochet any last-minute stitches, for squeeing with me at all the pretty, and for being the perfect editor in all ways imaginable.

Thank you to Steve Legato for the gorgeous photographs, to Kristi Hunter for the graceful prop styling, to Susan Van Horn for the lovely design, to Trina Dalziel for the beautiful illustrations—you guys. It's so pretty.

Thank you to Therese Chynoweth, without whom the patterns would be completely unreadable. Thank you to Kristin Kiser for having so much faith in me. Thank you to Anna Noyes, for being my extra brain and my extra fingers, and for making that basket about eighty times.

Thank you to my dad, who taught me (against my will) how to pun. Thank you to Kelly Notaras, Rachel Mehl, and Chandika Devi for being the sort of people, and forming the sort of company, that made it possible for me to do this. Thank you to Dave for holding my panicked hands when I lost my crochet hook on the plane. And thank you to Maile, who finally has her crocheted octopus.

# INDEX

# NOTES